Congrat's
Best wishes
for what's to come!
Happy cookin
Rock on!
Jack Allen
2016

LOCAL IN SOURCE

J

20 09

A

TEXAN IN SPIRIT

RESERVED
PARKING

JACK ALLEN'S
KITCHEN

Big Shoes to Fill

Jack Gilmore is the sort of person who lives by a few codes. In his daily life, he works hard to make sure he's delivering the best he can at his restaurants. For him, it's not just about great food. It's about taking care of his staff, looking out for the farmers he buys from, and ensuring his customers are having a great time.

I don't remember when I chose to follow him. He was just always leading. He never told me to work hard or move fast. I just did, because that's what he did. I knew that one day, I wanted to be in his shoes. And if you ask me, they're pretty big shoes to fill, especially when you are his son.

I started working for my dad when he was the head chef at Z Tejas, when I was 14. I did whatever they asked me to do, which basically included bussing and running food to tables. I hated it. I wasn't much for dealing with people back then—I much prefer to be behind the scenes.

After about a year, they let me in the kitchen to do prep and some event cooking. That's when I developed a passion for cooking. Until that time, I thought I wanted to be an architect. I loved designing things from scratch, and I spent countless hours at home, making models of houses and buildings with balsa wood. But the more time I spent in the kitchen, the more I fell in love with it. It still allowed me to be creative, but it involved much less math.

I remember hearing my dad tell people who wanted to get into the restaurant business to run the other way. It was just so much work, and if you didn't love it—really love it—you would be miserable. But when I told him I was thinking about it, instead of trying to talk me out of it, he took me on the road. At that time, Z Tejas was expanding across the country, so after high school, my dad taught me how to open restaurants. I spent more than a year going to places like Washington, Utah, and Maryland. I learned the basics of cooking; the ethics of being in a kitchen, being on your feet for hours, waking up early, and leaving late; and how to train new staff.

I also got to see my dad in his element. He's not always an easy guy to work for, especially if you're not quick to catch on to his way of doing things. He comes from a generation of cooks who yell a lot to get the results they want. But despite his rough edges, everyone who works for him respects him. I think it's because he's in the kitchen, rolling up his sleeves and working with them.

Jack is not hard on people just to be a jerk; he's hard because he wants things done right. He ran big restaurants with multiple locations and consistently good food and service. If there's one thing I took away from that year with him—aside from how to cook—it's that he's serious about how he wants his restaurants to run.

Once my dad realized he wasn't going to scare me out of the business, he took me to look at culinary schools. I ended up in San Francisco at the California Culinary Academy, where I learned new techniques and developed my own style of cooking. It's also where I learned the importance of sourcing food through local farmers and purveyors. In California, it's so easy to do. After school I worked in Aspen, where it's possible but much more challenging.

When I moved back to Austin, I brought my dad along with me to the farmers markets so we could get to know the growers and purveyors. Making those relationships allowed me to open my Odd Duck trailer, within a few days of the opening of Jack Allen's Kitchen.

While it was cool to grow up watching my dad help build Z Tejas, it was even cooler to see him open Jack Allen's. It's about all the things I've learned from him. He has opened a restaurant where he manages things on his own terms, from great food and loyal staff that you can depend on to warm hospitality and a commitment to supporting local farmers. What's more, he can focus on something that has meant a lot to him for a long time: giving back.

My dad does a lot, and not only for his family, staff, and guests. He gives time and energy to local causes. He goes out of his way to do things for people he doesn't even know. It's one thing I still need to take notes on. At some point, I hope I can make as much of an impact in that way as he has.

The best part about Jack Allen's Kitchen is Jack. It's that simple. It's not just a restaurant. It's a reflection of who he is. He's the one throwing the party every day, and everyone's invited. In the end, he's my dad. Some fathers and sons bond over baseball or football. I bond with my dad over the restaurant business. It's really rewarding to be able to look each other in the eye and have that conversation, knowing we're both living the same thing day in and day out. I'm proud of that.

BRYCE GILMORE
Chef/Owner, Barley Swine and Odd Duck

Jack's Story

On Saturday mornings, you'll find me at the farmers market. Actually, I go to a few of them throughout town. Most open at 9 a.m., and I'm usually standing right at the entrance by 8:45. At opening time, I move through the tents as if it were a timed competition. In some ways, it is. I'm not the only chef in Austin who likes to get an early jump on the best picks of the weekend. Plus, if you don't get there early enough, you have to compete with the general public, who are also hoping to find great ingredients.

I carry a roll of cash and four or five checks. When I first started doing this, I took more time, making a point to get to know each of the farmers who brought in the ripe heirloom tomatoes, the ears of sweet summer corn, and the heads of lush leafy greens. But now, it's about getting the best of what I can, so I can move to the next market. Nowadays I know the farmers and they know me. I know their spouses, their kids, even some of their pets. I've been to most of their farms and seen the great effort they put into their market tents each week.

When I'm making my rounds through the market, the farmers often know the bulk of what I want and have set it aside for me. That takes some of the thrill out of shopping, but realistically, they know I have more than 800 people to feed at my restaurants on any given day, and they know that Saturday mornings are short when you have a bounty of ingredients to sift through.

At farmers markets, I always ask farmers the same three things: How they are doing, how Mother Nature treated them that week, and if there's anything new that they've planted and I can get for my restaurants. It's relationship first and business second.

Each season brings a lot of the same ingredients from tent to tent. In summer you see squash, tomatoes, watermelon, peppers, and corn. In fall and winter, it's leafy greens, carrots, Brussels sprouts, and radishes. In spring, you find asparagus and green garlic, and I love to get my hands on the very first strawberries.

Saturday morning farmers markets are a ritual for me. I'm rarely able to stop at every tent, which means I often don't get to meet newcomers. But I do the best I can. Because I get there early, I like to rev things up. I'll buy 15 pounds of carrots from one guy and five pounds of cheese from another. It gives them optimism for the day and helps them out a bit.

By the time I have visited a few markets, my truck is full, my head spins with ideas for seasonal specials, the Texas sun is higher and blazing heat onto the market tents, and beads of sweat have formed along my brow.

I nod a few goodbyes to my farming friends and make my exit, knowing that our kitchen will probably see many of them later on. I tell every one that if they get stuck with produce at the end of market, knock on our back door. They know we'll put it to good use and we'll take care of them.

And in return, they always take care of us. That's how it was more than 100 years ago in upstart agricultural communities, and that's what we hope to preserve at Jack Allen's Kitchen.

JACK'S STORY

Though I consider myself a Texan, I was actually born in England. My mother moved my two brothers and me to Brownsville, Texas, when I was 3 years old. My home for my formative years was right on the border and right by the sea.

It was the early 1960s. My mother was a nurse, and she worked her ass off to take care of three boys. She worked a lot of nights. To help out, she had a Latina lady, Maria, come to live with us. Maria taught us Spanish and how to appreciate great Mexican food. She was amazing. We had fresh tortillas with every meal. On her days off, my brothers and I walked over to my aunt Mary's, just a few streets down, who was also an amazing cook. My mom could cook some too. I remember her chicken 'n dumplings and her fresh noodles, and her desserts were my favorite. But she really wasn't a major cook.

The summer when I was 15, I started busing tables at a steakhouse that also served fresh seafood. I had a good work ethic early on because I had watched my mother work her tail off for so long.

One night my boss had really had it with all the cooks, and he fired everyone in the kitchen except for one lady, Lupe. He told me to go help her. I had no idea what I was doing, but after spending time with Lupe, I learned a lot. She is the first person who taught me how to cook. She taught me how to put a steak on the grill, when to turn it, when to baste it with butter, and how to feel it for doneness. I really liked it.

When school started I could work only a couple nights a week because I played football. One night we were slammed at the bar, and my boss asked me to help out. So I started helping as a bar back, and before I knew it, I was serving beer and wine to customers. I loved it. I was surrounded by pretty waitresses and making tips left and right. It lasted for a few weeks. But it all ended when I asked for a Friday night off so I could play in our football playoff game.

My boss paused and looked at me. "Are you in high school?" he asked. "How old are you?"

"Sixteen," I said.

"Damn it," he said. "You may be one of the best 16-year-old bartenders I've ever seen, but you better get your ass back in that kitchen!"

I graduated in 1978 and went with my brother to see family in Pennsylvania for about six months. While I was there, I worked a flat top as a short-order cook at a diner serving up your typical eggs, bacon, and hash browns in the morning. I got used to having people shout orders at me. It was tough at first, but I learned how to do it pretty well. I also learned about farming communities. Everywhere we went had farmers markets with fresh ingredients from area farms. I'd never seen anything like that.

I liked Pennsylvania well enough, but I really wanted to be in Austin. I had hitchhiked there once when I was about 16 for a Willie Nelson Fourth of July picnic and fell in love with it. To this day, I have no idea where that picnic was, but after spending time at Barton Springs and walking around town, I knew it was where I wanted to be.

Once I got to Austin, I applied for a job at Shadows restaurant, a total rip-off of TGI Fridays, complete with a fern bar. It was run by two guys, Guy Villavaso and Larry Foles, who would later become two of my most influential mentors. I interviewed with Guy, who was a manager, maybe 24 years old, and I remember looking at him and thinking, "Man, I want to be a guy like that one day."

Guy asked for a reference, and I gave him the name of the steakhouse owner I worked for back home. My old boss told him that if he didn't hire me on the spot, he was an idiot. That rave review got me not only the job but also an increase in pay without negotiation.

I started in the kitchen and worked my way to kitchen manager within a few months. That was 1979, and I worked there a couple of years. Then we had an opportunity to open a French cafe concept at 29th Street and Guadalupe called Chez Fred. For years it was one of the top restaurants in Austin. I worked under Chef Robert Mayberry, who in the history of Austin chefs was one of the best in his time. He taught me the technical skills of a chef: how to make sauces, how to break down and butcher meat, how to slice bacon from pork belly. I give him a lot of credit for who I am now.

That was when I met my wife, LuAnn. Within a year we were married and had our first son, Bryce. To support our family, I had to get a second job. I started waiting tables at Louie's on the Lake in Westlake, a Cajun-inspired restaurant. It was easy tip money, and it allowed me to learn the other side of restaurants: the front of the house. I had the best of both worlds, and that's really how I learned the restaurant business. I lived it.

When LuAnn and I started thinking about a second child, we decided to move to her Hill Country hometown of Fredericksburg. I sold food to restaurants for a distributor for a while, but I hated it. So I had the bright idea to open my own restaurant. I was about 24, and honestly, I had no idea what I was doing. I lost my ass.

So I got a job at the German Bakery in Fredericksburg owned by George Zaranovic. I worked with him for about three years. He was truly a master chef. He knew everything about baking and traditional European cuisine. He taught me the art of putting flavors together and how to do base stocks, sauces, and marinades. My biggest regret is that I didn't spend more time on baking. I didn't have the patience for it. But I should have made the time.

A few years later, when Bryce was ready to go to school, we came back to Austin. I worked with Larry and Guy again for a while, but Chez Fred closed soon after. So I worked with restaurant owner Ronald Chang, who now runs Chinatown. He had a restaurant called El Chino on 6th and Brazos, across from the Driskill Hotel. It was an Asian-Southwest fusion concept that was the first of its kind anywhere. Chang taught me wok cooking, how to use high temperatures, and how to use Asian ingredients to interchange with flavors I already knew.

Around that time, Guy and Larry were working on a new restaurant concept on West 6th Street. It was in a total dump that was infested with bees, rats, raccoons, you name it. There was nothing else over there except Sweetish Hill. But Larry and Guy had a vision. And in 1989 they opened Z Tejas.

A satisfying catch of the day, on one of the first fishing trips I took to the Gulf Coast with my boys, Dylan, 5, and Bryce, 8.

PHOTO BY LUANN GILMORE

1
JACK

2
Jack Gilmore

3

4

5

6
Tyler's
AUSTIN, TX

I ended up becoming the head chef and created an entire menu from scratch that defined a new style of food in Austin. A lot of people called it Southwest cuisine, but I'm not really sure what that is. In the early 1990s, there really wasn't a definition for Southwest cuisine. And if you ask me, it's still undefined. Our food was influenced by everything from Mexican and Cajun to American and even Asian food. Whatever you want to call it, people were crazy about it.

Before long we had locations in Scottsdale and Las Vegas and another in Austin. I never imagined we would open more than a dozen locations, from Baltimore to Seattle. It was unreal. Early on at Z Tejas is when I met Tom Kamm, my business partner at Jack Allen's. He was with us as a general manager at first but later oversaw operations and corporate beverage buying.

My time with Z Tejas was like getting a master's degree in restaurants. I learned how to negotiate, design, and open full concepts. I learned how to streamline a kitchen so that each restaurant did everything the same way. It was invaluable experience. But in the back of my mind I always wanted to have my own place. Once I had been working with Tom a while, we started talking about doing our own thing. I had made a promise to LuAnn to get our kids through school first. So Tom and I waited a few years and stuck with the corporate job. But 20 years from the day I started with Z, I quit. Tom and I hit it off with a group of investors and opened Jack Allen's Kitchen in 2009.

Tom and I built the whole concept on what it's like to walk into our houses. The minute you are there, you are greeted with a drink and something to eat. That's just the beginning. We want to make sure you have a good time. Jack Allen's had to be fun and casual. We wanted people to feel like there are no strangers, that they could just pull up a chair and join in on the fun. Jack Allen's also had to be value-driven. We wanted our customers to feel like they could come in a few times a month without breaking the bank. (As it turns out, we have a lot of people who come in three and four times a week.)

It was also about doing things local. A lot of the inspiration came from watching Bryce, who was in culinary school in Northern California. Out there it was the norm to go to farms and find your ingredients, and he kept nagging me to start doing things that way. He is really the one to credit for that idea for Jack Allen's Kitchen.

I started going to farmers markets when we were ready to open. I said to the farmers, "You grow all the produce that you can for us, and I promise that if you show up at our back door, we will buy it from you." Once they understood that we were serious about it, Jack Allen's was ready to go.

We realized that to walk the walk we have to commit to the farmers, regardless of the ups and downs of working with Mother Nature. To this day, I get apologies every week from farmers, who say, "I'm sorry I couldn't get you what you really wanted this week," for reasons beyond their control, like too much rain or not enough rain or weevils or something. But I don't fault them for that. It's farming, and I'm not going to be an ass about it. Often I have to source it from another farmer, but they know we are here when their crop is back.

In many ways, it's not a gamble for us, because we know we can find what we need or adapt our menu to what we can bring in. It is a gamble for them. In the few years we've been open, and especially after opening our second location, a lot of farmers have added on to their crops just to keep up with the demand from our restaurant. So out of respect to them, we say, "You grow it, we'll use it."

To be honest, the restaurant is not 100 percent local. If we could source salmon from Texas, we would, but I doubt that will ever happen—or that it would be very good. There are just a few things we cannot get in Texas. However, I can point out the local products on just about every dish we serve and the farms from which they come. I would say we're consistently 70 percent or more locally sourced. Our tagline is real simple: Jack Allen's Kitchen Is Local in Source, Texan in Spirit.

When I quit Z Tejas, I let Larry and Guy know about our plan for Jack Allen's Kitchen. They were great about it, and it felt good moving forward with their support. Tom and I owed them for all they had done for us. We took that generosity and have invested it in our people at Jack Allen's. We feel we owe it to Austin's culinary community to develop the next group of people. Our hope with Jack Allen's Kitchen is to make more than just a great place to come and eat but to help create the next generation of great restaurateurs for Austin.

1 *Raising the sign at the second location of Jack Allen's Kitchen, in Round Rock.*

2 *Opening Z Tejas in Arizona and around the country.*

3 *Something I've spent most of my life doing, cooking over a hot flame.*

4 *Tom Kamm and I, opening the first Jack Allen's Kitchen, in Oak Hill.*

5 *A trip to Jalisco, Mexico, to watch how tequila is made. I am second from right, with (from left) a jimador agave worker, Doug Young, Ron Ryan, and Matt Dodson.*

6 *Cooking an invitational dinner at the James Beard Foundation House with a couple of culinary students, my sons Bryce and Dylan, and one of my head chefs, Chris TenEyck.*

#1 AND #6 BY LUANN GILMORE; #2 BY MIKE CURRAN; #4 BY SHANNON COLETTI.

Deep Eddy
Basil Bliss

Squash Blossom and Sweet Corn Soups

This soup is a nice base for a sweet spring or summer dish. When squash blossoms come in, around April, I like to use them for this because they have such color and a natural sweetness. To thicken the soup, use a little puréed potato. Use corn instead of squash blossoms when corn starts to come in, in late spring. We're usually able to get some early corn from our friends at Two Happy Children Farm. You'll need quite a few more blossoms compared with corn—about 3 times more—just to get the color and sweetness you're looking for.

SQUASH BLOSSOM SOUP (SERVES 4-6)

INGREDIENTS	MEASURE	CUT		PREPARATION
Squash blossoms	16 to 20		*Serve with Basil Oil (see page 38).*	(1) In stockpot on medium heat, simmer all ingredients together for approximately 20 minutes, until onions are tender. (2) Using hand-held mixer, blend soup until slightly chunky.
Zucchini	2 cups	Rough chopped		
Onion	1 cup	Chopped		
Heavy cream	2 cups			
Chicken broth (boxed is fine)	2 cups			
Garlic	2 tablespoons	Chopped		
Kosher salt	1 teaspoon			
Pepper	1 teaspoon			

SQUASH BLOSSOMS The squash blossom is used in a lot of dishes in Mexico and Italy. It is sweet, with a beautiful orange color. Farmers often overplant zucchini crops so that they can harvest blossoms to sell while they wait for the squash to develop. They package them up by the dozen and get $6 to $8, usually around the first part of April, just before we expect summer squash to come in. If you grow zucchini on your own and harvest the blossoms, just be careful to check inside for bees. My wife and I made the mistake of taking a bowl of about 15 of them into our house. We returned to the garden and came back to a house full of bees. They had been eating the nectar in the blossoms.

SWEET CORN SOUP (SERVES 4)

INGREDIENTS	MEASURE	CUT	PREPARATION
Onion	½	Chopped	(1) In large pot on medium heat, sauté onion, garlic, and parsley in butter until onions are tender, approximately 5 minutes.
Garlic	1 clove	Minced	
Parsley, fresh	¼ cup	Chopped	
Butter	1 tablespoon		
All-purpose flour	3 tablespoons		(2) Stir in flour, combining well, for 2 to 3 minutes.
Milk	2 ½ cups		(3) Whisk in milk and broth.
Chicken broth	1 cup		
Corn, fresh	6 ears	Kernels cut from cobs	(4) Add corn and cream cheese, and allow to heat through.
Cream cheese	2 ½ table-spoons		
Garlic salt	1 teaspoon		(5) Season, garnish, and serve.
Black pepper, ground	1 teaspoon		
Cayenne, ground	To taste		
Onions, green	For garnish	Chopped

Squash Blossom Soup with Basil Oil

Cured Salmon

MAKES 12 APPETIZERS

We go through a lot of salmon in a given week, butcher it in-house, and save as much as we can. So we cure a lot of salmon tail and belly to use as much of the meat as possible. The cured meat is good for things like a nice salad, a goat cheese spread, or salmon croquettes. This recipe in particular is one that I stole from Bryce after one of our Farmer Appreciation lunches.

INGREDIENTS	MEASURE	CUT		PREPARATION
Salmon fillet, skin on Kosher salt Brown sugar Black pepper	1 3 tablespoons 2 tablespoons 1 teaspoon	Scales removed Freshly ground		(1) On sheet pan, lay salmon skin side down and sprinkle with salt, sugar, and pepper.
Dill Tequila (save your best to drink)	1 good-sized bunch (save some for garnish) 2 shots	Roughly chopped, stems and all	** Open package every 12 to 24 hours and baste with accumulated juices.*	(2) Top with dill, splash on tequila, and wrap fish and sheet pan tightly with plastic; cover with sheet pan weighted with approximately 1 pound (like coffee can) and refrigerate for 2 or 3 days.
Goat cheese crumbles, your favorite Red onion Capers Dill	As needed As needed As needed As needed	 Thinly sliced		(3) On the second or third day, when fish has lost translucence, scrape off salt and other ingredients and slice thinly on the bias without skin. (4) For salmon rolls, place 1 tablespoon goat cheese on salmon slices, roll up, and garnish with red onion, capers, and dill.

SALMON Though we like to source as much as we can locally, there is no getting around the fact that you can't source salmon in Texas. (And I'm not sure we would want it if we could.) Salmon is such a staple for so many customers that we source it as responsibly as we can through our connection with Carol Huntsberger at Quality Seafood. Depending on the time of year or what is going on at fisheries around the world, it can be expensive too. We have prepared farmed salmon from Canada, Scandinavia, Scotland, you name it. When we can get it wild, that's even better, because it's so good.

For special dinners and events, we also have worked with a local purveyor named Sebastien Caillabet, of Celtic Seafare. He's half Irish, half French, and a trained chef from Le Cordon Bleu in Paris. He can get this specific hard-to-find Scottish salmon that he cures or smokes himself and sells through retailers and restaurants. We use his salmon when we need a large quantity and can't keep up with butchering it on our own. Caillabet has become a great trusted source in a pinch.

Grilled Asparagus with Red-Pepper Aioli

SERVES 6

This is a quintessential spring vegetable, and we can get it pretty readily in Texas. I prefer the thinner asparagus, about as thick as a pencil. The thicker kind is better for dicing up in a sauté or using in a soup. We trim off the last 2 inches, then toss the asparagus in olive oil, lemon juice, and salt and pepper and grill it up. You can use any dip, but I love something like Red-Pepper Aioli for its freshness.

GRILLED ASPARAGUS

INGREDIENTS	MEASURE	CUT	PREPARATION
Asparagus	20 to 30	1 ½ or 2 inches cut from ends	(1) Prepare grill. (2) In mixing bowl, toss together asparagus, onion, juice, and vinaigrette.
Red onion	1	Sliced	
Lime, fresh	1	Juiced	
Red Wine Vinaigrette *(see page 39)*	¼ cup		
Salt and pepper	To taste		(3) Place asparagus and onion on grill, season, and grill 1 to 2 minutes then flip and grill 1 to 2 minutes.

RED-PEPPER AIOLI

INGREDIENTS	MEASURE	CUT	PREPARATION
Roasted Garlic *(see page 273)*	½ cup		(1) In bowl, mix together all ingredients until smooth.
Mayonnaise, your favorite	1 cup		
Red bell pepper	½ cup	Roasted, peeled, seeded, and chopped	
Lime juice, fresh	2 tablespoons		

ASPARAGUS are abundant in Texas in the spring. The challenge is to harvest them pretty quickly because they can grow up to 4 inches a day when the nights are warm. This is a vegetable that really is at its best straight from the garden or from the farmers market. The longer it sits after being harvested, the more moisture and flavor it loses. Spears should be green from tip to end, with little or no white. Keep asparagus refrigerated in a plastic bag, and if you don't eat them the day you buy them, try this: Cut off the ends and stand them in an inch or so of water for about an hour before you cook them.

Quick Pickled Cucumbers

SERVES 6

There's something so refreshing about this as an addition to almost any dish. In the spring you have fresh dill, onion, and cucumbers. The perfect pickle size for a cucumber is 3 to 4 inches long, and you can either do it whole or as spears. If your cucumbers are much bigger than that, slice them up instead. The key is to submerge everything, and within in an hour, they are crispy with nice flavor. The best way to eat them is just as they are, but sometimes we'll fry them and serve them with Green Goddess dressing as an appetizer.

INGREDIENTS	MEASURE	CUT		PREPARATION
Cucumbers, the smaller the better	4 to 6	Sliced thin with mandoline or other vegetable slicer	**Pickled cucumbers will keep in refrigerator for up to 5 days.*	(1) In colander, toss cucumber with salt and let stand for approximately 30 minutes.
Kosher salt	1 tablespoon			
White vinegar	½ cup			(2) In medium saucepan, combine remaining ingredients and bring to boil; remove from heat and allow to cool. (3) Rinse salt from cucumbers and squeeze out as much moisture as possible. (4) Cover with pickling solution in medium bowl, and refrigerate 3 to 4 hours, covered, before serving.
Water	1 ½ cups			
Pickling spices, store-bought	¼ cup			
Sugar	1 cup			
Bay leaf	1			

Quick Pickled Cucumbers

Black-Eyed Peas

SERVES 4-6

Black-eyed peas are versatile: You can use them for Texas caviar or cook them up like a pot of beans. They also are creamy and have a great texture. This is a Southern-inspired recipe. You can throw ham in it or bacon and some jalapeño. My secret is that I finish it off at the last minute with vinegar and sugar, which just gives it a nice edge.

INGREDIENTS	MEASURE	CUT	PREPARATION
Bacon	4 to 5 slices	Chopped	(1) In 5-quart Dutch oven, cook bacon until crisp, remove, and reserve; leave bacon fat in pan.
Onion Celery Garlic	1 ½ cup ½ cup 4 cloves	Chopped Chopped Minced	(2) Add onion, celery, and garlic, and cook until tender, approximately 5 minutes.
Black-eyed peas, fresh Chicken broth (boxed is fine) Kosher salt Black pepper	4 cups 6 cups ½ teaspoon ¼ teaspoon	 Ground	(3) Add peas, broth, and seasonings, bring to boil, skim if necessary, and lower heat to simmer until tender, approximately 20 minutes. (4) Add bacon to pot and cook for 5 minutes.
White vinegar Sugar	2 tablespoons 1 tablespoon		(5) Add vinegar and sugar, adjust seasonings to taste, and simmer approximately 5 minutes.

Sun-Dried Tomato Basil Vinaigrette

MAKES 4 CUPS

In this dressing for spring salads, the basil is sweet and balances nicely with the tomato. But you have to be careful. Because of its sweetness, the dressing is not good on just any lettuce, like iceberg or romaine. It's better with lettuce that has a little spiciness to it, like arugula or a field mix. Classic sweet-and-spicy love affair.

INGREDIENTS	MEASURE	CUT		PREPARATION
Sun-dried tomatoes Water	1/4 pound 1 quart			(1) In stockpot on high heat, boil tomatoes in water to cover for 1 minute; drain and cool.
Basil, fresh Balsamic vinegar	1/2 cup 2 cups	Stemmed		(2) In blender, blend tomatoes, basil, and vinegar until slightly chunky.
Olive oil	1 1/2 cup		**Vinaigrette will last in refrigerator for up to 3 weeks.*	(3) While blending, very slowly add oil to emulsify, and blend well.

Basil Oil

MAKES 3 CUPS

This is the perfect spring add-on for dishes because it's fresh and vibrant and it brings out unexpected flavors from the other ingredients. Drizzle it over soups—it looks pretty—and use it as a finishing oil. Or just slice a few nice heirloom tomatoes and top with a little Basil Oil. It's heaven.

INGREDIENTS	MEASURE	CUT		PREPARATION
Olive oil Basil, fresh Garlic Lime juice, fresh Kosher salt and cracked black pepper	2 cups 2 cups 4 cloves 3 tablespoons To taste	 Stems removed	**Oil will last in refrigerator for up to 3 weeks.*	(1) In blender on high, add oil, then add remaining ingredients and blend well.

Red Wine Vinaigrette

MAKES 4 ½ CUPS

It's always good to have a staple dressing on hand, and that dressing is even better when it's homemade. This is my standard versatile dressing for just about any salad. If you want a creamy version, simply mix in an equal part Ranch dressing, and there you have it.

INGREDIENTS	MEASURE	CUT		PREPARATION
Red onion Dijon mustard Basil, fresh Balsamic vinegar Black ground pepper	¼ cup ½ tablespoon 1 ounce 2 cups ½ tablespoon	¼ inch diced Stemmed		(1) In blender, combine first 5 ingredients until slightly chunky.
Egg Olive oil, or your favorite vegetable oil	1 2 cups		**Vinaigrette will last in refrigerator for up to 2 weeks.*	(2) Add egg and oil to mixture, and blend well.

Cucumber Relish

MAKES 2 CUPS

This is your picnic or patio-dinner salad that really showcases the cucumber in spring and summer. You have to be careful about your cucumbers, though. When they get too dry, they are bitter and not worth using. We buy more cucumbers than we need at the restaurant. Before we use them, my staff tastes the first slice. If it's bitter, we throw the whole thing out. That means we throw away about 30 percent of our supply, but it's better than serving a bitter dish or cocktail.

INGREDIENTS	MEASURE	CUT	PREPARATION
Red onion Cucumber Cilantro Rice wine vinegar Olive oil White sesame seeds	¼ cup 1 cup 2 tablespoons 2 tablespoons 2 tablespoons 2 tablespoons	Chopped Peeled, seeded, and chopped Chopped	(1) In mixing bowl, combine all ingredients well and reserve for ramen noodles *(see page 45)*.

FRESH@
75
QUALITY
SEAFOOD
MARKET
1938-2013

QUALITY SEAFOOD

AS TOLD BY CAROL HUNTSBERGER

I BELIEVE EVERYTHING in life happens for a reason. When you take advantage of the opportunities that come along, you will be amazed where life takes you. How else would you explain a blond cosmetics saleswoman from Dallas taking on a struggling seafood business and becoming a fish expert? It may sound out of the ordinary, but as they say, stranger things have happened.

After a chapter of my life raising children while working as a sales director for Mary Kay Cosmetics, in 2003 I took a leap of faith with my husband at the time and bought Quality Seafood Market. It was more than just an everyday market. Quality Seafood had an extensive history in Austin that began in 1938, when Garnett Lenz first opened as part of John Stan's Fruit and Vegetable Market at 11th and Congress, across from the state Capitol. Since then the market has changed hands and locations a few times, but the mission remained the same: to bring the freshest quality seafood to the Austin area.

We took over from the company's third owner, Sam Eaves, who had run the business since 1990. Before that, Chester Hasted and his family ran it for 32 years, after Hasted purchased it from Lenz, in 1958.

My husband, Paul, and I had no experience with wholesale or retail, and we certainly didn't know anything about the seafood industry. Paul had spent most of his career in the financial services industry and was looking for a change. At first I swore I would have nothing to do with it. I was happy selling makeup, raising children, and playing tennis three times a week. But a year into it, we were losing money and we began to think we had made a mistake.

I had an accounting degree, so I took a look at the books. I committed to at least turn things around and build the business to the point that we would have something to sell. But the truth is, once I got my hands into everything, I fell in love with it. Within two years we went from losing money to receiving our first paycheck. Soon after, Paul and I parted ways, and I took over the market completely in 2010. I have never looked back.

Of course, I had a significant learning curve, and the people who work here taught me everything I know. Lee Chandler, our retail manager, has been here for 23 years. My wholesale manager, John Martinez, has been here 36 years, and Tom Cantu, who used to be our general manager, has been with us since 1960. Although he retired from his managing job, he still comes in a few days a week to work the phones. I would have been lost without him.

I've spent the past few years fostering relationships with a whole Rolodex full of people we buy from. Depending on the seasons and types of fish we want, we have a number of people from around the world who get us what we need. Sometimes I work with a co-op of fishermen, sometimes it's the fisherman directly. Other times our vendors are groups that harvest farm-raised fish. And then there are larger companies that work as middlemen and represent smaller companies.

Early on, I went down to the Gulf Coast several times to visit my vendors. The Gulf is one of our primary sources of fish, and I wanted to know everyone and see the operations for myself. I was so green back then that I couldn't identify the majority of fish coming through our doors. But people like Tom Cantu taught me everything. Now I can tell how good a fish is by sight, touch, texture, and cut.

Another thing I learned was that we have the same challenges farmers do.

Another thing I learned was that we have the same challenges farmers do. Mother Nature can effect any number of changes on our oceans and fisheries in a given year. I constantly gauge how certain natural events—from hurricanes and droughts to floods and red tides—will affect my ability to get the fish I'm looking for. And that doesn't even skim the surface of man-made challenges we face, like overfishing and oil spills.

I try to spend a few minutes

QUALITY
SEAFOOD

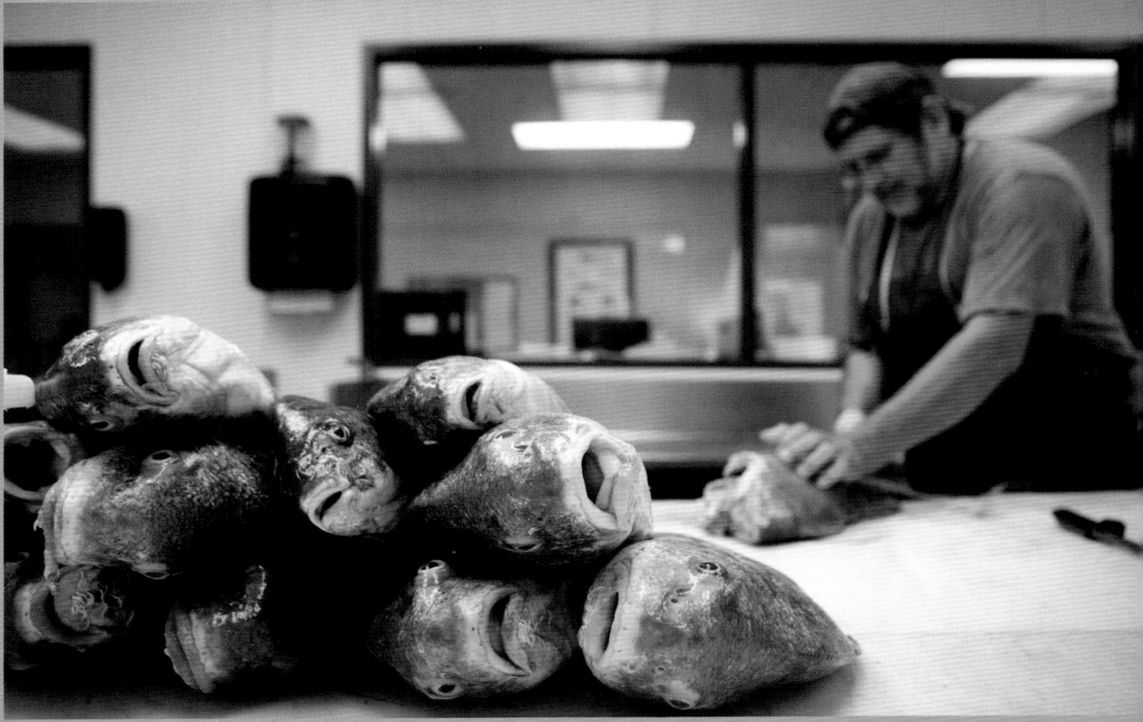

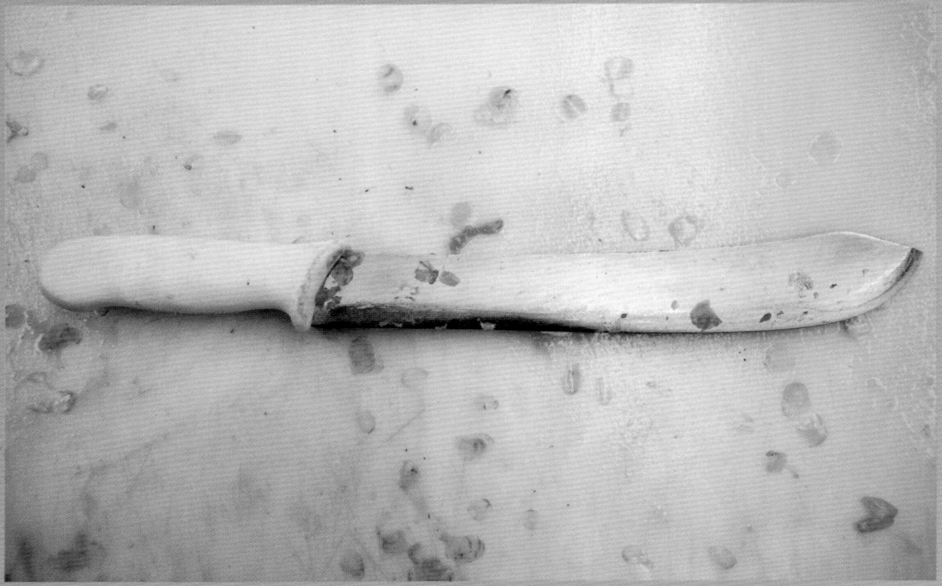

with our fisherman when they come in. They know better than anyone else what's going on out there. They know the winds, the rains, the temperatures, and the meaning of it all. They didn't learn it from books; they're part of generations of fishermen who have lived it for years and years. I trust what they know. I have to—because it's that information that I sift through to know what I'll have for my clients and customers.

Quality Seafood Market is three businesses in one. We have an onsite restaurant and grill as well as a retail counter for walk-in customers, which account for 50 percent of the business. The third business is wholesale to restaurants. That's the side of the business that can get tricky, especially when we have trouble sourcing fish that a restaurant needs or when we get fish that doesn't meet our standards. But honestly, it's the problem solver in me that likes to deal with those challenges.

I'm a member of so many seafood organizations I can hardly count. I'm on the Shrimp Marketing Board for the Texas Department of Agriculture, and I'm involved with the Atlantic and Gulf Fisheries Group and the Parks and Wildlife associations for a number of states. When I get to work every morning, I have more than 40 emails with updates on all the different fisheries.

I've worked with Jack Gilmore for years, long before Jack Allen's Kitchen. And it's been one of the most rewarding business relationships I've had. He's a great mentor, business partner, and friend. Clients like him make me want to do the best I can to get the best product at a good price. And if I can't get him what he needs, I work my tail off to find the next best solution.

The past few years have been a bit of a whirlwind but one of the best experiences of my life. We purchased an entire building to allow for a complete remodeling. Now we have 16,000 square feet, double what it used to be. That has allowed us to expand our dining room and build an additional seafood bar. Plus, we brought in a 1,700-square-foot cooler and built a spacious cutting room so we can better serve our wholesale business.

These days I eat fish at almost every meal and I often find myself working six days a week. But I know I'm getting the best seafood I can to some of the best restaurants in the city. Not bad for a girl who couldn't tell the difference between sockeye salmon and ruby red trout more than a decade ago.

This is what we at Jack Allen's Kitchen love to see coming in from Quality Seafood. We'll find a way to serve this up for one of our evening specials.

Kimchi Stew with Tuna and Ramen Noodles

Snow Pea Stir Fry

Kimchi Stew with Tuna and Ramen Noodles

SERVES 3-4

This is a dish we came up with on a trip to the Bahamas. I was with Tom and my chef Chris TenEyck for a few days of fishing. It's a different ballgame than fishing on the Texas coast. It was fun, but I'm not a huge fan of trolling around at 18 miles an hour. We didn't actually catch any tuna, but we did get some mahi mahi and some wahoo. We smoked those and made a nice broth with them. Then we added ramen noodles and a slaw of carrots and cucumber. We served it with some lime and hot sauce, and it was just delicious.

INGREDIENTS	MEASURE	CUT	PREPARATION
Toasted sesame oil	1 tablespoon		(1) In pot on medium high, heat oil and stir-fry kimchi and garlic for approximately 5 minutes.
Spicy Kimchi (see page 34)	2 cups	Chopped in 1-inch pieces	
Garlic	1 teaspoon	Minced	
Water	3 cups		(2) Add water and broth to pot, and bring to hard boil.
Kimchi broth, the juice from your jar of kimchi (see page 34)	¼ cup		
Ramen noodles (discard soup mix)	1 packet		(3) Cook noodles until almost done, 2 minutes. (4) Add tuna and scallions, and cook 2 more minutes.
Tuna, fresh	6 ounces	Chopped	
Scallions	3	Trimmed and cut into ½-inch pieces	
Cucumber Relish (see page 39)	As much as you want: refreshing		(5) Serve with relish.

Grilled Gulf Shrimp Salad with Greens, Strawberries, and Watermelon

Fried Fish with Sweet and Spicy Avocado Sauce

Crunchy Fried Shrimp with Blackberry Sauce

Fried Fish with Sweet and Spicy Avocado Sauce

SERVES 3-4

The best reward for a long day of fishing is a plate of crispy fried fish. It might seem intimidating to set up a fryer, but go on. It's easy and worth it. I like to serve this dish with Sweet and Spicy Avocado Sauce instead of your regular ol' tartar or cocktail. Although, come to think of it, there's nothing wrong with that either.

FRIED FISH

INGREDIENTS	MEASURE	CUT		PREPARATION
Buttermilk Eggs	2 cups 2			(1) For buttermilk wash, in bowl whisk together buttermilk and eggs.
Seasoned Flour *(see page 191)* Panko breadcrumbs	2 cups 2 cups			(2) For breading mixture, in bowl blend flour and breadcrumbs.
Fish fillets, your favorite (redfish, snapper, etc.)	1 to 2 pounds	2 inches by 3 inches	**Fry in batches; do not crowd.*	(3) Prepare electric fryer or stove-top fryer to 350 degrees. (4) Dip fillets in buttermilk wash, dredge to coat well in breading mixture, and place in fryer; shake after 30 seconds so fillets do not stick together. (5) Fry 3 to 4 minutes until crispy and golden brown, and drain.
Sweet and Spicy Avocado Sauce *(below)*	As much as you want			(6) Serve with sauce.

SWEET AND SPICY AVOCADO SAUCE (MAKES 3 CUPS)

INGREDIENTS	MEASURE	CUT	PREPARATION
Avocado	2	Skinned and seeded	(1) In mixing bowl, mash together avocado and dressing, and season to taste.
Baja Dressing *(see page 270)*	1 cup		
Salt and pepper	To taste		

Crunchy Fried Shrimp with Blackberry Sauce

SERVES 3-4

Everyone loves fried shrimp, right? They are crunchy, salty, and sweet, the perfect bite to pop in your mouth. For dipping, instead of cocktail sauce, use a seasonal ingredient, blackberries, for spicy Blackberry Sauce. You'll still taste the horseradish, but you get the sweet and tart berry as an accent.

INGREDIENTS	MEASURE	CUT		PREPARATION
Buttermilk Eggs	2 cups 2			(1) For buttermilk wash, in bowl whisk together buttermilk and eggs.
Seasoned Flour *(see page 191)* Cracker meal	2 cups 2 cups			(2) For breading mixture, in bowl blend flour and meal.
Shrimp	16 to 20	Peeled, deveined, and butterflied	**Fry in batches; do not crowd.*	(3) Prepare electric fryer or stove-top fryer to 350 degrees. (4) Dip shrimp in buttermilk wash, dredge to coat well in breading mixture, and place in fryer; shake after 30 seconds so shrimp does not stick together. (5) Fry approximately 1 ½ minutes until crispy and golden brown, and drain.
Blackberry Sauce *(below)*	As much as you want			(6) Serve with sauce.

BLACKBERRY SAUCE (MAKES 1 ½ CUPS)

INGREDIENTS	MEASURE	CUT	PREPARATION
Blackberry preserves Horseradish Dijon mustard Soy sauce	1 cup ¼ cup ¼ cup 3 tablespoons		(1) In bowl, combine all ingredients together well.

GULF COAST SEAFOOD

FROM AN EARLY AGE, I was influenced by the Gulf of Mexico and the Rio Grande Valley region. The Gulf was everywhere. Most of my friends had dads who fished for a living—or just for fun—and brought fresh redfish and snapper and crab home all the time. As kids we were always at the water. Sometimes we just played around in the sand while the dads fished. Sometimes they gave us chicken necks to put on crabbing baskets. I loved pulling those baskets up and seeing all those crabs latched on to the chicken bones.

One summer, when I was about 15, I went shrimping with one of my friends on his dad's commercial boat. It was one of those big 30-year-old wooden boats, with paint stripping off, manual cranks on the fishing gear, and one tired old air-conditioning unit in the bunk galley. No comforts of home. But I really wanted to see what it was like to be a fisherman.

On a shrimp boat you work at night and sleep in the day. We put out the nets just before dark and trolled for a few hours. You'd be out there at night and have no idea where land was, nothing but pitch black and stars. Just before daylight, we pulled in the nets. I remember the first time I saw a net hit the deck. It just exploded with shrimp pouring out all around us.

If you're lucky, most of the nets come back like that. If you're unlucky, you net the bycatch. Of course, the captain wanted only the shrimp, but I thought it was pretty cool to pull in stuff like sharks or trash fish, license plates, beer bottles, tires, and stuff like that. It was like a treasure hunt.

I learned how to sort the shrimp. We threw big and medium shrimp into separate tanks and the smaller ones back in the water. The first shrimp I ever saw had heads on them. When I started cooking for a living, I thought it was weird to see shrimp without heads.

Sometimes, when we had a break, they boiled some shrimp and made a quick Mexican cocktail, with tomato juice, chile sauce, and fresh lime. Citrus was a staple on the boat. And when you're out there floating in what seems like the middle of nowhere, it's the best thing you've ever tasted.

On that trip, we were scheduled to be out four or five days, but we came in early because we were full. I didn't go back out after that. I realized pretty quickly that I wanted to stick around on land, chase girls, and make money. But to this day, when I'm shopping for shrimp, if it's not from the Gulf, I won't buy it. That trip made me respect what fishermen do. And it made me appreciate the quality of seafood we have from the Gulf.

It's something people might take for granted, but the Gulf of Mexico is such a plentiful source of amazing seafood, and it's right in our own backyard. These days I spend as much time as I can down there, not as much as I'd like, but if a few months go by and I haven't been fishing, I get antsy. I pack up the truck with a few friends, and we hit South Padre, Rockport, or some other little fishing town. We rent a house, hire a guide, and get on the water for as long as we can. It's an escape. It's like going on vacation and going back to my roots all at the same time. And it helps me keep a good perspective on the bounty of fish we have available to us.

At the restaurant, we rely primarily on one person to source the best seafood for us. That's Carol Huntsberger of Quality Seafood Market in Austin. She's our go-to person for all of our seafood, Gulf Coast or otherwise. She gets ruby red trout from Idaho and salmon from all over the world, depending on what's sustainable and available. Carol works to get us what we need and can deliver it straight to us. She also is good about calling me when she has something that she thinks we might want to use so I have a chance to buy it first.

Taco con Todo

SERVES 4-6

As a kid, I liked to head to the beach with my friends for fishing or surfing. Afterward, we would stop at a small taco stand that served up these killer breakfast tacos called "taco con todo," or taco with everything. Some people stop with egg, bacon, and cheese for a breakfast taco, but what's wrong with putting on everything you like? Add beans, potatoes, meat, lettuce, and tomato to that, and you have a breakfast that will stick with you for most of the day.

INGREDIENTS	MEASURE	CUT	PREPARATION
Eggs	4	Beaten	(1) Heat large nonstick skillet with cooking spray on medium until hot, and scramble eggs until almost done. (2) Add meats, potato, and pico.
Sausage patties	2	Cooked and chopped	
Bacon	4 slices	Cooked and chopped	
Potato, baked and cooled	1	Chopped	
Pico de Gallo *(see page 98)*	¼ cup		
Flour tortillas	4		(3) To make tacos, sprinkle each tortilla with ¼ of cheese, top with ¼ of eggs, then fold over, pressing gently. (4) Heat large nonstick skillet with cooking spray on medium until hot, and cook tacos until cheese melts, 1 to 2 minutes per side. (5) Cut into wedges and serve with Pico de Gallo.
Cheese	1 cup	Shredded	

Braised Lamb Shanks

German Potato Salad

Pot Roast with Potatoes, Turnips, and Carrots

Black-Eyed Peas

Pot Roast with Potatoes, Turnips, and Carrots

SERVES 6

So many people serve this dish in the spring for Easter Sunday, but really it's a peasant sort of dish. It's about taking a lesser cut of meat, like the beef shoulder, and braising it for a couple of hours to make it tender and flavorful. The key is to sear the meat on the stovetop in the pan you plan to use for the braise. Every mom or grandma has her go-to roasting pan, so if you're new to the game, get one and stick with it so that time after time, it just makes your roast better and better. To me the best part of pot roast happens the next day. You already have gravy and good, flavorful vegetables. You can make a soup or stew with it. Or you can do what my mother-in-law did. She cut it up in a grinder with homemade pickles and then finished it with good mayo on toast for a killer sandwich.

INGREDIENTS	MEASURE	CUT	PREPARATION
Vegetable oil	2 tablespoons		(1) Preheat oven to 350 degrees.
Beef chuck roast or your favorite roast (bone in gives more flavor)	5 pounds		(2) In large Dutch oven or large roasting pan, heat oil over medium-high heat, season roast on all sides, and brown all sides, approximately 10 minutes.
Kosher salt	1 teaspoon		
Black pepper	½ teaspoon		
Beef broth (boxed is fine)	2 cups		(3) Turn meat fat side up, and add broth, wine, vegetables, and herbs.
Red wine	½ cup		
Onions	3	Cut into large wedges	
Celery	1 cup	Chopped	
Garlic	4 cloves	Chopped	
Dried bay leaves	2		
Dried thyme	1 teaspoon		
Tomato paste	2 tablespoons		(4) Stir in tomato paste, bring to a simmer, then roast, covered, for 2 hours.
Potatoes	2 pounds	Cut into 1½-inch chunks	(5) Add vegetables, and cook until tender, approximately 1 hour.
Turnips	1 pound	Cut into 1½-inch chunks	(6) Transfer roast and vegetables to platter, and skim fat from pan juices. To serve, cut roast in thick slices, serve with vegetables, and pass pan juices separately.
Carrots	2 pounds	Cut into 1½-inch chunks	

Braised Lamb Shanks

SERVES 6

Lamb is something you think of in the spring. We usually use lamb from Twin County Dorpers out of Harper, in the western Hill Country. We start out by braising the shanks for about an hour in a mirapoix (a mix of onions, celery, and carrots), tomatoes, spices, and some wine. We cover it and just let it cook. Then we purée the liquid and remove the fat for a perfect stock. Serve it with Chunky Potato Mashers *(see page 279)*.

INGREDIENTS	MEASURE	CUT	PREPARATION
Lamb shanks	6, approximately 5 pounds		(1) Sprinkle shanks with seasonings.
Salt and pepper	To taste		
Olive oil	2 tablespoons		(2) In heavy large pot on medium high, heat oil. (3) In batches, brown shanks until brown on all sides, approximately 8 minutes per batch; transfer to bowl. (4) Sauté vegetables in pot until golden, approximately 10 minutes.
Onions	2 cups	Chopped	
Carrots	3 large	Peeled, cut into ¼-inch rounds	
Celery	2 cups	Chopped	
Garlic	10 cloves	Minced	
Dry red wine	4 cups		(5) Stir in remaining ingredients, and return shanks to pot, pressing down to submerge. (6) Bring to boil, then reduce heat to medium low, cover, and simmer until meat is tender, approximately 2 hours. (7) Uncover, simmer until very tender, another 30 minutes, and transfer shanks to sheet pan. (8) For sauce, using immersion blender purée remaining ingredients for a chunky sauce.
Diced tomatoes with juices	28-ounce can	Chopped	
Chicken broth (boxed is fine)	2 cups		
Beef broth (boxed is fine)	1 cup		
Rosemary, fresh	5 teaspoons	Chopped	
Thyme	2 teaspoons	Chopped	
Lemon peel	2 teaspoons	Grated	

Enchilada Tejana

Blackened Fish Enchilada

Enchilada Tejana

SERVES 2

Is it lunch or breakfast? When you add a fried egg to something, eat it whenever you want. You can make this dish more like a casserole or as individual enchiladas, but I like it as the former. Bake it all together in a dish and then pop 6 or 8 fried eggs on top before you serve it for that extra richness.

INGREDIENTS	MEASURE	CUT	PREPARATION
Heavy cream Jack Allen's Salsa *(see page 99)*	2 cups 2 cups		**For Ranchero Cream Sauce:** (1) In saucepan simmer cream and salsa until thickened, 10 to 15 minutes.
Corn tortillas Corn oil	6 ¼ inch deep in skillet		**To soften but not cook tortillas:** (2) Using tongs place tortillas in hot oil in skillet, turn almost immediately, then hold to drain.
Chicken Tinga *(see page 283)*	2 cups		(3) Preheat oven to 500 degrees. (4) On oven-safe serving plates, create enchiladas: lay down tortilla, add spoonful Ranchero Cream Sauce, and add ⅓ cup Chicken Tinga. Repeat for stack of 3, and cover with Ranchero Cream Sauce. (5) Bake approximately 5 minutes, until bubbly.
Eggs	2		(6) Fry eggs in skillet with oil from softening tortillas, place one on each enchilada, and serve with black beans and Veggie Studded Rice *(see page 227)*.

Blackened Fish Enchiladas

SERVES 6

This is the sort of dish you get after fishing on the coast because it serves a lot of people after a long day on the water. Some restaurants will take your fresh catch, grill it up, and serve it in enchiladas. Most of the components for this dish are already used for other recipes in this book. We like to add a nice Sweet and Spicy Avocado Sauce *(see page 54)* to it, just for a little more flavor.

INGREDIENTS	MEASURE	CUT	PREPARATION
Carl Miller's Chunky Queso *(see page 104)* Jack Allen's Salsa *(see page 99)* Milk	2 cups 2 cups 1 cup		**To make Tejana Sauce:** (1) In saucepan combine queso, salsa, and milk and simmer for approximately 5 minutes; reserve.
White fish, your favorite Salt and pepper	1 pound To taste		**To blacken fish:** (2) Heat cast-iron skillet to medium high, and season fish on both sides. (3) Cook 2 to 3 minutes on each side (it's okay if it flakes apart); reserve.
Corn tortillas Corn oil	6 ¼ inch deep in skillet		**To soften but not cook tortillas:** (4) Using tongs place tortillas in hot oil in skillet, turn almost immediately, then hold to drain. (5) Preheat oven to 500 degrees. (6) On oven-safe serving plates, create enchiladas: lay down a tortilla, add spoonful Tejana Sauce, and top with flaked fish. Repeat for a stack of 3, and cover with Tejana Sauce. (7) Bake approximately 5 minutes, until bubbly, and serve with black beans and Veggie Studded Rice *(see page 227)*.

(512)
SANYO
STASH
IPA
INDEPENDENCE BREWING CO.
PECAN
PORTER
Thirsty Planet
BREWING COMPANY
THIRSTY GOAT
AMBER
THIRSTY GOAT
TEXAS RED
Rahr & Sons
FORT WORTH TEXAS
AMBER LAGER

TEXAS BEER

AS TOLD BY TOM KAMM

When we were building out the Jack Allen's Kitchen in Oak Hill, we had only four beer taps designed into our bar. We were working on our bar program around the same time Thirsty Planet Brewery released its first beers. One day, a guy wanted me to taste beer in a van out in the parking lot. I said, "Really?" So I went out to his van, where he had kegs of all his beers, and we started tasting through them. I thought they were really good. I asked him where else he sold his beer, and he said, "Nowhere." So we gave Thirsty Planet Brewery its first tap. I think we became its first invoice. And Thirsty Goat Amber Ale became our first Texas beer on tap.

Since then, so many Texas beers are available that I can hardly keep track. According to the Brewers Association, Texas is the second largest per capita consumer of beer in the country. Right now, it ranks 42nd for the number of breweries per capita, thanks to strict production and distribution laws. But things are starting to change.

The 2013 legislative session included new laws that allow production breweries to sell pints and bottles of beer for consumption on the premise of the brewery. Previously, those packaging breweries could charge for a tour, offering tastes of beer for guests, but could not formally charge for the sale of beer like in a bar.

Breweries classified as "brewpubs" are a hybrid of restaurant and brewery that sell 25 percent or more of their beer on site. The new law now allows brewpubs to sell beer to go as well as distribute to off-site accounts.

Based on Texas's growing number of breweries poised to open doors in the coming years, we are slated to catch up with states like New York, Oregon, and Colorado. In a recent economic study from the University of Texas at San Antonio, the Texas craft brewing industry had a $608 million impact on the state as of 2012. With continued changes in beer laws such as the ones recently passed, the study estimates that the growth of the industry could reach $5.6 billion within the next decade.

In Austin alone there's a lot of beer to celebrate. Live Oak Brewing Company has been brewing great pilsner and hefeweizen since 1997 and was the first to attract attention about local beer. On a larger scale, Real Ale Brewing Company out of Blanco puts out a wide portfolio of beers that are distributed statewide, including the Fireman's #4 blonde ale that sells like crazy in the summertime. And then there's Jester King Craft Brewery, which is perhaps one of the most unique breweries around here, making artisanal-style beers often with local wild yeasts. Its beers are a little pricey to sell at the restaurant, but they are a pleasure to drink.

Among the other breweries in Austin, it's hard to settle on a favorite. Austin Beerworks and Independence Brewery both put out solid beers. We also like the Mexican-style beers out of Twisted X Brewery, and the guys over at Hops and Grain Brewery actually worked with us years ago at Z Tejas. Alt-eration pilsner and Zoe pale ale lager, from Hops and Grain, are both standard beers in my home refrigerator. 512 Brewing Company rounds out the list with a handful of really good beers. Its Pecan Porter is amazing with a scoop of Amy's vanilla ice cream as a creamy dessert treat.

Now is definitely a good time for the Texas beer industry. My only regret is that we don't have more taps for more Texas beers. Had we been able to see into the future of Texas beer, we would have planned differently.

Chocolate Icebox Cake with Chocolate Ganache

SERVES 8-10

We all need a good standard chocolate cake recipe. I've been taught different ways to keep it moist. People use mayonnaise or sour cream, but how about banana? That's the key ingredient for our pastry chef, Dee-Dee Sanchez. It's just enough to keep things moist, but you can't even taste it. Everyone has an opinion about how to serve cakes, but I think room temperature makes it taste best. That's kind of a problem for a restaurant because we make things in such large quantities that you have to preserve it by keeping it cold. If you chill it, our best solution is to serve it with ice cream, which isn't a bad answer to a good cake at all.

INGREDIENTS	MEASURE	CUT		PREPARATION
Bananas Eggs Vanilla, Mexican Canola oil Butter Water Sugar	3 6 1 tablespoon 1 ½ cups 2 ounces 3 cups 6 cups	Very ripe Chopped Hot		(1) Spray 3 9-inch-round cake pans with cooking spray and line bottoms with perfectly fitting parchment paper. (2) In large bowl with stand mixer and paddle attachment or hand mixer, blend bananas and next 6 ingredients until creamy.
All-purpose flour Salt Baking soda Baking powder Cocoa powder, unsweetened	4 ½ cups 1 tablespoon 1 tablespoon 1 tablespoon 2 ¼ cups			(3) In separate bowl, combine flour and next 4 ingredients, then add slowly to wet ingredients, scraping bowl with spatula, until well integrated; pour batter evenly among pans.
Pecans, Texas Chocolate chunks White chocolate chips	¾ cup ¾ cup ¾ cup, plus more as needed to decorate with drizzle	Chopped	**Cakes are done when centers spring back slightly when touched, soft but not mushy.*	(4) Sprinkle each cake with ¼ cup each pecans and chocolates, and bake approximately 30 minutes. (5) Cool completely in pans, turn out, peel off parchment, and set aside.
Heavy cream Honey, Texas	5 cups 6 ounces			**For ganache icing:** (6) In saucepan whisk together cream and honey, then over medium-high heat watchfully bring to boil.
Dark chocolate chips, or quality semisweet chocolate Bourbon	2 ¼ pounds As needed, for added moistness and flavor		**Ganache is ready to use when spreadable. It may be made a day ahead, refrigerated, then brought to room temperature for several hours for perfect consistency.*	(7) In large bowl place chocolate, pour cream mixture over it, and whisk briskly until thoroughly melted; allow to cool in refrigerator, stirring occasionally with spatula.

ASSEMBLY:

(1) Invert one layer of cake onto serving platter, and brush surface with bourbon.
(2) Spread approximately 1 cup ganache evenly and out to edges, about ½ inch thick.
(3) Add next layer, and repeat with bourbon and ganache; top with final layer, and brush with bourbon.
(4) Refrigerate for approximately 30 minutes.
(5) Melt remaining ganache in microwave oven or double boiler. It should not be too hot; room temperature is best for more coverage.
(6) Pour ganache over edges of cake slowly, and let it run down sides.
(7) Fill in top to cover completely.
(8) Drizzle with melted white chocolate in random streaks.
(9) Chill until ready to serve.

Raspberry Muffins with
Brown Sugar Streusel
Blackberry Cobbler

Blackberry Cobbler

SERVES 8-10

Blackberries come out in late spring and early summer. Taste the fruit before you bake, because if it's really sweet, you can scale back a little on the sugar. Early in the season the fruit may be more tart so you'll need more sugar to balance them out. You can use this recipe for a mix of berries or other seasonal fruit throughout the year, like peaches and apples.

INGREDIENTS	MEASURE	CUT	PREPARATION
Blackberries, fresh Brown sugar Sugar Cinnamon Vanilla	4 to 5 pints ½ cup ½ cup 1 teaspoon 1 teaspoon		(1) Preheat oven to 350 degrees, and spray a 10- or 12-inch-round cast-iron skillet with cooking spray or rub with oil. (2) Toss blackberries with sugars, cinnamon, and vanilla, and pour into skillet.
Butter, chilled Sugar Brown sugar All-purpose flour	8 ounces 1 cup 1 cup 3 cups	Cut into pieces	**For streusel topping:** (3) In large bowl using two forks, mix and mash up butter with sugars and flour until crumbly and loose, then pour over blackberries. (4) Bake for approximately 45 minutes until evenly browned, and serve warm, with vanilla ice cream or fresh whipped cream.

Raspberry Muffins with Brown Sugar Streusel

SERVES 12

Raspberries are hard to get in Texas. But when we're low on blackberries, we source raspberries or blueberries from California or Mexico. With raspberries, these muffins are a real treat. The recipe works with just about any berry or fruit, like peaches in summer and apples in fall, with a dash of cinnamon and nutmeg.

INGREDIENTS	MEASURE	CUT	PREPARATION
All-purpose flour	2 cups plus 1 tablespoon		(1) Preheat oven to 350 degrees, and spray muffin tin with oil or use cupcake liners. (2) For muffin batter, in medium bowl, whisk together the first 5 ingredients. (3) Add in oil, applesauce, and eggs, and do not overmix.
Baking soda	1 teaspoon		
Baking powder	½ teaspoon		
Salt	½ teaspoon		
Sugar	⅔ cup		
Canola oil	½ cup		
Applesauce	1 ¼ cup		
Eggs	2		
Raspberries, fresh	½ pint or more		(4) Fill muffin cups ⅔ full and top with a few raspberries.
Butter, chilled	4 ounces	Cut into pieces	**For streusel topping:** (5) In large bowl using two forks, mix and mash up butter with sugars and flour until crumbly and loose, then top each muffin with 1 tablespoon of streusel.
Brown sugar	¼ cup		
Sugar	¼ cup		
All-purpose flour	1 cup		
			(6) Bake for 15 minutes and serve warm.

Red Velvet Cake with Strawberries in Mason Jars

SERVES 8

This is a variation on strawberry shortcake but with a rich red velvet cake. When I see strawberries, I know we are done with winter and I am ready for spring. In a good year, we mainly get our strawberries from Oak Hill Farm in Poteet, which is a town renowned for them. But when Oak Hill Farm is not able to get us all we need, we have other farms that do a great job as well.

INGREDIENTS	MEASURE	CUT	PREPARATION
Beet	1		**For beet purée:** (1) Roast beet wrapped in foil at 400 degrees 45 minutes to 1 hour, depending on size, until fork tender; cool slightly, and wearing rubber gloves rub off skin with towel. (2) In blender, purée with 2 to 3 tablespoons water until smooth; cool to room temperature. (2) Preheat oven to 350 degrees, and spray inside of 9 x 12 sheet pan with cooking spray and line bottom with perfectly fitting parchment paper.
Canola oil All-purpose flour Sugar	2 1⁄4 cups 1 pound plus 2 ounces 1 pound		(4) In bowl of stand mixer with paddle attachment, combine 1⁄4 cup beet purée with oil, flour, and sugar.
Baking powder Baking soda Cocoa powder Buttermilk Vanilla White vinegar	1 teaspoon 1 1⁄2 teaspoon 3 tablespoons 1 1⁄2 cups 2 tablespoons 1 1⁄2 teaspoon		(5) In medium bowl, sift together powder, soda, and cocoa, then add next 3 ingredients and mix completely. (6) Pour buttermilk mixture into beet mixture, and mix slowly until incorporated.
Eggs	3		(7) Add eggs and mix just until combined; do not overmix. (8) Bake approximately 20 minutes, until center springs back when touched; set aside and let cool.
Cream cheese Butter, unsalted	1 pound 4 ounces	Softened Softened	**For cream cheese icing:** (9) In bowl of stand mixer with paddle attachment mix cream cheese and butter on medium for 5 minutes; scrape sides and mix 1 minute.

CONTINUED

INGREDIENTS	MEASURE	CUT		PREPARATION
Powdered sugar Vanilla	1 cup 1 tablespoon			**Cream cheese icing continued:** (10) Add sugar and vanilla, mix 2 to 3 minutes until a bit more fluffy, and set aside.
Heavy cream Honey, Texas	4 ounces 1 tablespoon			**For ganache:** (11) In saucepan whisk together cream and honey, then over medium-high heat watchfully bring to boil.
Dark chocolate	8 ounces	Chopped		(12) In large bowl place chocolate, pour cream mixture over it, and whisk briskly until thoroughly melted; set aside and allow to cool.
Heavy cream Sugar Mexican vanilla Strawberries, fresh Texas	2 cups ¼ cup ½ teaspoon ½ pint	 Sliced	**Prepare whipped cream right before assembling jars so it doesn't deflate.*	**For whipped cream:** (13) In bowl of stand mixer with whisk attachment, mix cream, sugar, and vanilla until medium peaks form.

ASSEMBLY:

To assemble 8 mason jars, using cookie cutter, cut 16 rounds of red velvet cake, and place 1 in bottom of each jar. Spoon or pipe in approximately 1 ½ tablespoons cream cheese icing and add 3 or 4 slices strawberry. Add 1 tablespoon cream cheese icing, top with cake round, and cover with 1 tablespoon ganache. Cover with lids and refrigerate until serving, or top with whipped cream and strawberries and serve immediately,

SUMMER

Cucumber-Jalapeño Rita

SERVES 4

Traditionally, cucumber and lime go really well together. I remember, when I was a kid, squeezing lime and shaking paprika on cucumbers and eating them. And, of course, lime and tequila go really well together. So why not make it a threesome? We source the best cucumbers and remove the seeds to keep the cocktail from getting cloudy. With jalapeño, it's usually about the kick, but here, we use the chile more for flavor than for heat. We take out all the seeds, so it's not spicy at all.

INGREDIENTS	MEASURE	CUT		PREPARATION
Cucumber	1	Peeled, sliced into 1/4-inch slices, seeds removed		(1) In 32-ounce mason jar or lidded container, muddle cucumbers with simple syrup.
Simple syrup *(see page 18)*	6 ounces			
Lime juice	6 ounces	Fresh squeezed	**We like Ambhar, Z Tequila or Dulce Vida.*	(3) Add lime juice and remaining ingredients except cilantro. (4) Close lid and shake 10 times; refrigerate.
Reposado tequila	8 ounces			
St-Germain Elderflower Liqueur	4 ounces			
Jalapeño	1	Sliced into 1/4-inch slices, seeds removed	**Leave the seeds in the jalapeño for even more heat.*	
Cilantro	1 bunch			(5) Pour rita over ice in 10-ounce glass, and garnish with cilantro sprig.

Manor Punch

Manor Punch

SERVES 4-6

We came up with the name for this punch because we use White Hat Rum, which is made east of Austin, in Manor. The rum has a lot of Texas molasses in it and is aged four months in oak, which gives it an overall unique characteristic. It adds a little complexity to a punch like this. Summer melons are just right for rum punch, and this is the perfect cocktail to make in a large batch for a summer party by the pool.

MELON ICE CUBES (MAKES 12 CUBES)

INGREDIENTS	MEASURE	CUT	PREPARATION
Watermelon, cantaloupe, and honeydew melons, seedless	6 cups	Peeled and chopped	(1) Place fruit in blender or processer and blend, adding water as needed, until smooth. (2) Strain through China cap strainer, pour into 2 large silicon ice trays (6 cubes to a tray), and freeze overnight.

PUNCH

INGREDIENTS	MEASURE	CUT	PREPARATION
White Hat Rum	8 ounces		(1) In small punch bowl, combine all ingredients including Melon Ice Cubes. (2) Pour into tumblers, with at least one Melon Ice Cube per glass, and serve.
Luxardo Maraschino Liqueur	2 ounces		
Lime juice, fresh squeezed	2 ounces		
Lemon juice, fresh squeezed	2 ounces		
Ruby Red grapefruit juice, fresh squeezed	6 ounces		
Bar Keep Lavender Bitters	4 to 6 dashes, to taste		
Melon Ice Cubes	8 to 12		

Texas Whiskey Shandy

SERVES 4

We developed this drink to incorporate more Texas whiskies into our cocktail program. The guys making TX Blended Whiskey are doing a good job with it, perfect for the heat of summer. I needed something refreshing to go well with this whiskey, so I came up with a twist on a shandy, which is typically made with beer. We used local honey and figs for a syrup that adds another dimension to the flavor and cider for effervescence and tartness.

ROUND ROCK HONEY-FIG SYRUP

INGREDIENTS	MEASURE	CUT	PREPARATION
Water	32 ounces		(1) Bring water to boil and add next 2 ingredients. (2) Reduce heat and simmer for 15 minutes, stirring occasionally. (3) Strain out figs, and set aside to cool.
Round Rock Honey	8 ounces		
Figs, dried, from Boerne, Texas	1 cup	Sliced	

SHANDY

INGREDIENTS	MEASURE	CUT	PREPARATION
Lemons	2	Sliced into 6 wedges each	(1) Hand squeeze lemons and drop into pitcher. Add syrup and whiskey, and stir. Pour over ice into Collins or tall glasses.
Round Rock Honey-Fig Syrup *(see recipe above)*	5 ounces		
TX Blended Whiskey (Firestone & Robertson Distillery, Fort Worth)	9 ounces		
Apple cider, your favorite	6 pack or 750-mililiter bomber; approximately 3 ounces per drink		(2) Top each glass with cider. Stir with spoon, add straw, and garnish.
Sliced figs and lemon twists	For garnish		

Texas Whiskey Shandy

Fresh Blackberry Mojito

SERVES 1

Blackberries in the summer are fantastic, and we wanted a cocktail to showcase them. Mojitos are easy and fresh. We use ingredients you can take from your garden, like summer mint and blackberries. White rum gives a cleaner, fresher taste and works perfectly for a summer patio drink.

INGREDIENTS	MEASURE	CUT	PREPARATION
Simple syrup (see page 18)	1 ounce		(1) In 12-ounce Collins glass, gently muddle first 4 ingredients until skin of fruit is broken and all juice is extracted. Do not overdo, as mixture will become bitter.
Blackberries, fresh	3 or 4, plus 1 for garnish		
Lime	½	Cut in quarters	
Mint leaves	5 medium size, plus 1 for garnish		
White rum	1 ½ ounces		(2) Fill glass with ice, add rum, top with soda water, and stir with bar spoon. (3) Garnish with blackberry and mint leaf.
Soda water	3 to 4 ounces, as a top off

FARM TO TABLE

SOME OF LIFE'S most pivotal inspirations come while driving a car, and that was the case with John Lash. The seasoned marketing exec had played out his corporate gig in Austin and couldn't shake the desire to cut a new career path. But he had no idea what that was. While he cruised the rolling hills of Capital of Texas Highway, it hit him: a farm-to-restaurant delivery business.

Full disclosure: Lash pinched the idea from a National Public Radio story about a Michigan food broker, selling produce from famers to restaurants. Within a week, Lash booked a trip to meet the guy and shadow him for a few days. It was the perfect answer to a very real problem. Texas farms are rich with beautiful seasonal food year-round. Chefs need that food in their kitchens. Lash could make it possible.

When he returned home, he launched Farm to Table, a fresh food delivery business. "In Texas, there's a 12-month growing cycle. There's never a time when there isn't something great to eat in this state," says Ohio-born Lash. "I knew there would be more traction for a business like this in Texas than in Michigan, so I went with it."

The idea of using local ingredients had become a prevalent philosophy for most of Austin's leading restaurants. But not all chefs have the luxury of shopping farmers markets every Saturday.

So what's a chef to do? Call John Lash.

At first, the idea took time to grow. Lash visited markets across Central Texas, striking up conversations with each of the farmers. Bit by bit, he gained a healthy list of farmers interested in supplying their produce to his business. His appeal among Austin chefs took a grassroots approach as well.

"After certain farmers started to get to know me, I got calls from other farmers," says Lash. "When I asked how they heard about me, they said, 'So-n-So told me I needed to work with you,' and it just grew from there."

Lash and his son, Sam, began the delivery process by driving a 150-mile route each week in a beat-up truck without air conditioning, depositing Farm to Table produce on chefs' kitchen doorsteps. To grow that clientele, they made up samplers of local produce in brown paper sacks and scattered them to a few restaurants on Saturdays. Eventually, word caught on, not only on the restaurant scene but among farmers as well.

"I remember when John and his son showed up at our kitchen door with a brown bag of produce," says Jack Gilmore, who was working at Z Tejas. "It's guys like Lash that made me realize I wanted to do a restaurant of my own completely differently. I wanted to support local farms. I wanted to support him. Period. When we started Jack Allen's Kitchen, we made a relationship with him for life."

Since 2008, Farm to Table has bridged the mileage and time gap between chefs and farmers. Lash now has a few more trucks—with air conditioning—and a larger staff that covers hundreds of miles through Central Texas each week, bringing fresh vegetables, fruits, meats, and cheeses to eager chefs. Most people call him the middleman, but if you ask just about any Austin (or San Antonio) chef who works with Lash, they call him a godsend.

"He helps us immensely," says Gilmore. "We wouldn't have half the Texas ingredients without him. We just can't do that on our own. We still make an effort to have direct relationships with local farms. That's important to me. But John makes our goals for this restaurant possible."

"We wouldn't have half the Texas ingredients without out him. We just can't do that on our own."

Today Lash's radio-sparked inspiration has taken root. His cell phone perpetually buzzes with calls, texts, and emails. He sends weekly email updates to clients about the batch of goods he will have on deck. That email roster once was 30 or 40 clients strong; now it's well over 500 in Austin and San Antonio and throughout the Hill Country, including Jack Allen's Kitchen.

"John's got our backs, all the time," says Gilmore. "He stores the last of anything he has for the season just for us. He knows we'll find a way to use it. He buys it at an honest wage and marks it up enough so he can make some money out of it too, and I honestly don't worry about his prices. I just want to know how much I can get."

ORVIS
FR-AC-16173
NT DB

ITZ
GARDEN

Smashed Guacamole

SERVES 2-4

Making guacamole can tell a lot about a person. Back in the day, I added sour cream because I wanted it extra creamy. But these days, I keep it simple. You don't want to overthink it. I personally like it chunky. You can't go wrong getting a big hunk of avocado when you scoop it with a chip. We don't use a whisk; we just rough cut the avocado with a spoon and stir in the pico de gallo, salt, and pepper. If you cut everything else right, the easiest part is adding the avocado. The best way to serve guacamole is fresh, as fresh as possible. We make ours to order so you get the absolute best of the ingredients. We smash it up, sprinkle it with cotija and roasted pumpkin seeds, and call it good.

INGREDIENTS	MEASURE	CUT	PREPARATION
Avocados, ripe	2	Cut in half, peeled, and pitted	(1) Smash avocado, pico, and seasonings together to form a chunky dip.
Pico de gallo *(see recipe below)*	½ cup		
Kosher salt	¼ teaspoon		
Black pepper	¼ teaspoon		
Cotija	2 tablespoons	Grated	(2) Top with cheese and seeds, find your favorite chip, and dig in.
Pumpkin seeds, roasted	2 tablespoons		

PICO DE GALLO (MAKES 3 CUPS)

INGREDIENTS	MEASURE	CUT	PREPARATION
Tomatoes	2 cups	¼-inch diced	(1) In glass bowl, mix all ingredients together well.
Onion	½ cup	¼-inch diced	
Jalapeño	2 tablespoons	Seeded and minced	
Cilantro	1 tablespoon	Chopped	
Lime, fresh	½	Juiced	
Olive oil	1 tablespoon		
Salt and pepper	To taste		

Jack Allen's Salsa

SERVES 2-4

Everyone likes a good salsa. We wanted ours to be memorable, and not just for its flavor. We roast the tomatoes and tomatillos with other spices and purée half of it to make it more of a sauce. Then, before serving, we combine both the sauce and the chunky portion in a mason jar and shake it table-side for our guests. That adds a frothiness for enjoying on the spot. The recipe asks to purée the whole thing, but if you like chunky salsa like I do, reserve half for a quick chop and add that to the puréed portion.

INGREDIENTS	MEASURE	CUT	PREPARATION
Tomatoes, ripe and plump Tomatillos	3 2	 Shucked	(1) Preheat oven to broil. (2) Place tomatoes and tomatillos on sheet pan, and roast until skin blisters.
Guajillo chiles, dried Onion Water	2 ¼ cup 1 cup	 Chopped 	(3) Place tomatoes, tomatillos, chiles, and onion in water in pot, and boil for 10 minutes.
Garlic Onion salt Salt and pepper	½ tablespoon 1 teaspoon To taste	Chopped	(4) Add all ingredients to blender, purée until slightly chunky, and season to taste.

Smashed Guacamole

Jack Allen's Salsa

Carl Miller's Chunky Queso
Tomatillo Salsa

Carl Miller's Chunky Queso

SERVES 4-6

Queso is a Texas staple. We had to have it on the menu. Ours is pretty standard, with Velveeta cheese, pico de gallo, milk, and peppers. That's right, I use Velveeta. I realize it's a bit of a departure from the philosophy of using local farmed ingredients, but it melts the best and gives the best result. We also like to add a scoop of guacamole and our Green Chile Pork to give the appetizer a little more heft, but you don't have to. The best thing about our queso is that it's served for a good cause. We've supported the Lone Star Paralysis Foundation for years, and a portion of the sale of each order of queso we serve benefits the foundation.

INGREDIENTS	MEASURE	CUT	PREPARATION
Velveeta (Yes, that's right. I admit I love Velveeta.)	2 pounds		(1) In a saucepot on low heat, melt cheese, stirring constantly so it doesn't burn.
Pico de Gallo *(see page 98)* Milk Adobo sauce, from chipotle pepper	1 cup 1 cup 2 tablespoons		(2) Stir in remaining ingredients, and get your chip on. *For the real Carl Miller's Chunky Queso, add a scoop each of Smashed Guacamole *(see page 98)* and Green Chile Pork *(see page 286)*.

QUESO FOR A CAUSE

Before I opened Jack Allen's Kitchen, my wife, Luann, and I were looking for a charitable cause that we could really get behind. We wanted to give back to the community that had been so good to us. My friend Doug English, an All American UT and All Pro Detroit Lions football star in the 70s and 80s, had started a charity a while back called the Lone Star Paralysis Foundation. His NFL career came to an end due to a spinal cord injury, and upon meeting Kent Waldrep, who played for the TCU football team, English became inspired to help Waldrep and others recover from spinal cord injuries. Through his foundation, he raises money to fund research, recovery therapy, and recreational wheelchair programs.

Each year, the foundation hosts an auction event, and in 2005, I offered to auction off a dinner that I would cook for 8 to 10 people. English suggested we host it at the Governor's Mansion, with a tour and then this nice dinner. I liked the idea, so I agreed to it.

The next year at the auction, LuAnn and I were seated at a table with strangers, including Carl Miller, who runs an oil and gas staffing company in Central Texas. Even though we didn't know each other, we all had this great vibe together, like we had been friends for a long time. When my item came up for bid, I noticed this guy Carl raising the price: $1,300, $1,500, and so on.

I tapped him on the shoulder and said, "Do you know you're bidding on me?" He said, "No kidding?" and then he kept raising his hand. $2,000. $2,500. And he won it.

The following year, we set the same item for the same amount of people, this time hosted at English's house. Carl made the winning bid again. Each year, it just got bigger and bigger. It got to the point that each year, Carl was bidding upwards of $15,000.

Over the years, all of us at that table have become really good friends. And it became Carl's thing to win this dinner. A couple of years ago, I decided to offer up two dinners. Someone was always in a bidding war with Carl, and I figured we could raise more money if I just did a dinner for the top bids. So we got my son Bryce involved to help me cook, and the first year we raised more than $30,000 for the two dinners. It was amazing.

When we opened Jack Allen's Kitchen, we wanted to do more. So we picked an appetizer that would promote the Lone Star Paralysis Foundation. We named it after Carl Miller because he stepped up and bought every auction dinner from the very beginning. We could have picked a random appetizer, but we wanted one that people would identify with, and who in Texas doesn't love queso? Carl Miller's Chunky Queso is one of our top five sellers, and $1 from every order goes to the Lone Star Paralysis Foundation in honor of Carl.

We probably raise more than $10,000 a year from queso at the Oak Hill restaurant. With the second restaurant in Round Rock, we've doubled that. And with our new location, in Austin on Capital of Texas Highway, we're raising even more. The other thing we do is a tequila dinner in January that raises more than $15,000. Combining funds from the main auction, the queso sales, and the tequila dinner, we probably raise more than $60,000 annually for the foundation.

But the best part about working with that group is the people. The board is dedicated, and the doctors who work with the organization do so much on their own dime to further the cause. The foundation relies heavily on volunteer participation, with less than 4 percent of the money raised going toward payroll. That means more money goes to the mission. Countless times at fundraising events, a patient has been present and is able to stand or to walk, when he or she couldn't before, all because of the work of the foundation.

Until we find a cure for paralysis, Carl Miller's Chunky Queso will be on the Jack Allen's menu—and for all the right reasons.

Each year we hold a fundraising dinner for the Lone Star Paralysis Foundation at Jack Allen's Kitchen. Partying with us are Doug and Claire English (at left) and Deanna and Carl Miller.

PHOTO COURTESY HOLLY JACKSON AUSTIN AMERICAN-STATESMAN

Tomatillo Salsa

MAKES 3-4 CUPS

We like to use this salsa for specials and events. On their own, tomatillos can be really acidic, so they need help. When you roast them and add a little chicken broth, they are ready to work with a lot of different ingredients. They stay a little tart and make a great canvas for jalapeños, cilantro, and lime. The key is to find the right size, not too big. Golf-ball size is what you're looking for or you don't get the flavors you need.

INGREDIENTS	MEASURE	CUT	PREPARATION
Tomatillos, whole Onion	5 ½ cup	Husks removed Chopped	(1) Preheat oven to broil. (2) Place tomatillos and onion on sheet pan, and roast until skin blisters.
Vegetable oil Chicken broth (boxed is fine)	1 tablespoon 1 cup		(3) Heat oil in saucepan on high until it just starts to smoke. (4) Stir tomatillos and onion in oil and broth, and set aside to cool.
Garlic Kosher salt Black pepper	2 tablespoons 1 teaspoon 1 teaspoon	Chopped	(5) Blend together tomatillo mixture with remaining ingredients until smooth.

TOMATILLOS I love tomatillos. They are such a versatile ingredient once you know how to use them, like in sauces for enchiladas and fresh fish. A lot of people think tomatillos are green tomatoes, but they're not. They're actually related to gooseberries.

Tomatillos are in a husk, similar to corn. Peel them and clean them with just water, and then you have a nice canvas. From there you can add some acid or heat like a jalapeño and then an herb like cilantro, or maybe even oregano, and then you make a little salsa out of it.

Or introduce it to fire, like the oven broiler, and let the skin blister a little bit, which brings out a different level of flavor. I also love to throw them on the grill to add a little smokiness. When you get the color you want from the blistering, you'll also notice the juices start to come out, which is exactly what you're looking for. Take them off the heat, and start making your sauces or salsas.

Pimiento Cheese

MAKES 8-10 MASON JARS

When I was growing up, we went to an old steakhouse where they served a little crock of cheddar cheese spread and saltine crackers. I wish I could remember the name of that restaurant because it's what inspired us to greet customers with this at Jack Allen's Kitchen. It's customary to get chips and salsa at Tex-Mex restaurants, and Italian and fine dining restaurants present diners with bread and butter or olive oil. We wanted to serve something unique. Something that was Southern and Texan in spirit. The homemade Pimiento Cheese gets people talking the second they are seated. It is a slam dunk. It costs a lot to do it, but it would cost more not to. And it means a lot to our staff to greet customers with something complimentary. It's just a little taste, but if you want more, just order a portion from the menu. I've been surprised by how many people have come around on pimiento cheese. They say, "Jack, I hate pimiento cheese, but I love yours." This recipe makes quite a bit. But if you're going to put in the effort, you may as well make enough to last a couple of weeks. Plus it makes a great gift to bring over to neighbors or friends.

INGREDIENTS	MEASURE	CUT	PREPARATION
Cream cheese, softened	½ pound		(1) Whisk together all ingredients in mixer, and store in refrigerator until ready to use. (2) Serve with Navajo Bread *(see page 221)* or chips, on sandwich bread, or however you want.
Monterey Jack cheese	½ pound	Grated	
Cheddar cheese	½ pound	Grated	
Mayonnaise	1 cup		
Red bell pepper	1 cup	Roasted, seeded, and chopped	
Worchestershire sauce	1 teaspoon		
Sherry vinegar	1 teaspoon		
Kosher salt	½ teaspoon		

BELL PEPPERS Everyone who plants bell peppers wants to harvest green bell peppers. They're a little bitter and really crunchy, and they add a good bite to Louisiana-style recipes like creole, gumbo, and jambalaya. But what's even better is when the sun gets on the peppers and they ripen up. That's when they become sweet and red, which is what we look for in the peppers we use for our Pimiento Cheese. We try to get as many as we can from whatever farms have them.

Pickled Peach and Pine Nut Relish

SERVES 4-6

This is a recipe I stole from my son Bryce. He has used it at a few events, and it's always well received. Pickling the peach is what I like the most. Sometimes you get peaches in summer that aren't quite ripe and don't have the sugars you're looking for. But I don't feel right about throwing them away, so pickling them is a perfect solution. Pine nuts really make this recipe pop, but the dish would also work with pecans. Serve the relish on fish, chicken, or pork, and it's even great as a dip with tortilla chips.

INGREDIENTS	MEASURE	CUT	PREPARATION
Fennel seeds	½ teaspoon		(1) Place first 7 ingredients in 10-inch skillet and roast for 3 to 4 minutes, until aromatic.
Cumin seeds	½ teaspoon		
Coriander seeds	½ teaspoon		
Mustard seeds	½ teaspoon		
Red chile flakes	½ teaspoon		
Black peppercorns	½ teaspoon		
Bay leaves	5		
Water	2 cups		(2) Add water and sugar to spices, let steep for 4 minutes, remove from heat, and reserve. (3) Boil medium saucepot of water, blanch peaches for 30 seconds, and immediately shock in ice bath. (4) Peel, pit, and cut into wedges. (5) Place peaches in shallow bowl, pour pickling liquid over them through mesh strainer, and let stand for 2 hours.
Sugar	1 cup		
Peaches	4 to 5	Shallow X cut in bottom of each	
Pine nuts, roasted	½ cup	Chopped	(6) Drain peaches, add remaining ingredients, and toss well.
Shallots	2 tablespoons	Chopped	
Parsley	½ cup	Chopped	
Olive oil	½ cup		
Salt and pepper	To taste		

HILFIGER
NO ONE LOVE
A SOLDIER

Chile Purée Sauce (Hot Sauce)

MAKES 6-7 CUPS

Chiles are abundant in summer. And that's a good thing. I ask the farmers I buy from to get me as many as they can to make this purée. I don't age it like Tabasco does, but I do go through a similar process to make it. I source both green and red chiles and keep them separate—otherwise you just end up making an ugly brown sauce. The greens are the hottest, the reds a little sweet. Basically we introduce three simple ingredients: vinegar, salt, and water. We cook it, purée it, and strain it. It goes with just about anything you want to heat up a little. Usually we pour it into shaker bottles and put them on the table with dishes like eggs, enchiladas, and meatloaf. For home use, just repurpose a liquor bottle from your bar.

INGREDIENTS	MEASURE	CUT		PREPARATION
Green or red jalapeños	4 cups	Clean, whole, with stems removed	**You need to wash the peppers really well. I dip them a few times in hot salted water for 10 seconds.*	(1) Combine all ingredients in large saucepan, and bring to boil over high heat for 1 minute. (2) Transfer to blender and pulse with lid on. **Do not purée immediately as heat could cause mixture to explode from blender.** (3) Remove lid and allow steam to escape. (4) Replace lid and purée completely. (5) Strain through sieve into jar, and store in refrigerator.
Water	6 cups			
White vinegar	2 cups			
Kosher salt	2 tablespoons			

New Mexico Green Chile Sauce

MAKES 10-12 CUPS

These chiles are mainly associated with New Mexico, but I love their flavor. They are harvested in July and August, the hottest time of the year, which also means they are particularly spicy. We roast them first and use them for sauces, and this one is the special ingredient in our Green Chile Pork *(see page 286),* a staple in our street tacos lineup. Use it for rellenos, enchiladas, or breakfast tacos. We made this recipe for a big batch. It freezes beautifully, and you can parcel it out throughout the year.

INGREDIENTS	MEASURE	CUT		PREPARATION
Anaheim peppers	3 pounds			(1) Roast peppers in broiler on large sheet pan until skins begin to blister, approximately 5 minutes. (2) Remove and cover with plastic to sweat, for approximately 10 minutes. (3) Peel and seed.
Water	5 cups			(4) Place water and peppers in gallon container, use immersion blender to purée, strain through sieve, and set puréed liquid aside.
Canola oil Yellow onion	½ cup ½ cup	 Chopped		(5) In gallon stockpot, sauté oil and onion on medium heat for approximately 4 minutes.
Flour Garlic	3 tablespoons 3 tablespoons	 Minced		(6) Whisk in flour and garlic, stirring vigorously to avoid clumps, for 2 minutes.
Kosher salt	1 teaspoon			(7) Add salt and puréed ingredients to onion mixture, and cook on low heat for 8 minutes, stirring regularly.
Baking soda	1 teaspoon		** This may foam up a lot so that's why you need to use an oversized pot.*	(8) Add baking soda to de-acidify, cook 2 more minutes, allow to cool, and store in airtight container in refrigerator.

Jack

MILAGRO FARMS

WE BUY A LOT of our eggs from Milagro Farms, a family farm run by Kris and Amy Olsen in Red Rock, southeast of Austin. I met Kris at the farmers market when I first started Jack Allen's. He's a character who is kind of hard to miss. He's tall, with long curly blond hair, and he's always wearing a big smile. Considering he's originally from Southern California, he's what you get when you cross a surfer with a farmer. He and his family used to run a really big farm on the West Coast, but they eventually sold it to downsize and move to Texas.

They grow a number of vegetables that I sometimes pick up, like lettuce, green garlic, onion, and bell peppers, but Milagro's prize ingredient for me is its eggs.

Early on, I aligned myself with Kris, giving him all of my egg business. A few times, when he's had a shortage, I've had to go find eggs elsewhere, but I've tried to remain loyal to his farm.

When we first opened up Jack Allen's, we had deviled eggs on the daily menu. But they were a pain to do every day. It's harder than you think to boil and shell a bunch of eggs perfectly. It's particularly hard to do that with fresh eggs. You just can't peel them. Kris told me an egg has to be somewhere between 14 and 21 days old for it to peel properly. There are tricks, like putting salt or vinegar in the water, running eggs under cold water, this and that. I don't care what you do, it's still a bitch to peel.

With eggs from the grocery store, you'll be fine because those eggs are usually older. But we get ours fresh from Kris, and we don't have the space to store them for two weeks at a capacity that allows us to serve them every day. So we just serve them for our Sunday brunch, and that seems to keep everyone happy.

We use eggs in dressings, salads, entrées, and brunch items. And these days we'll put a fried egg on top of just about anything, from our Enchilada Tejana, to shrimp and grits, to a big juicy burger.

Deviled Eggs

SERVES 6

Deviled eggs are just a classic Southern comfort food. Most people repurpose the yolk with a little mayonnaise and relish, but there's nothing wrong with using homemade pickles and some sort of protein like chorizo, andouille sausage, lobster, or shrimp. It's like an egg salad sandwich without the bread.

INGREDIENTS	MEASURE	CUT	PREPARATION
Egg yolks	6	Mashed	(1) Use a fork to combine all ingredients. (2) Get your devil on, and fill up your eggs.
Mayonnaise	2 tablespoons		
Apple cider vinegar	1 tablespoon		
Dijon mustard	1 tablespoon		
Green onion tops	2 tablespoons	Minced	
Red bell pepper	1 tablespoon	Minced	
Parsley	1 tablespoon	Chopped	
Salt and pepper	To taste		

HOW TO: BOIL EGGS

When it comes to peeling a bunch of farm-fresh eggs, it's usually a pain in the butt because the shells don't always come off nicely. But I learned a trick from a friend at the Salty Sow restaurant in Austin, something her grandmother used to do, and grandmothers are usually right. I tried it and sure enough, it works!

(1) Place eggs in saucepan in single layer. Add cold water to cover by 1 inch. Heat on high just to boiling. Remove from burner and cover.
(2) Let eggs stand in hot water 9 minutes for medium eggs, 12 minutes for large eggs, 13 minutes for extra-large eggs.
(3) Drain and cool completely under cold running water or in bowl of ice water, then refrigerate.
(4) Boiled eggs are easiest to peel after cooling, which causes the egg to contract slightly in the shell. Gently tap egg on countertop until shell is finely crackled all over. Roll egg between hands to loosen shell. Start peeling at large end, holding egg under cold running water to help ease off the shell. Slice eggs in half lengthwise and separate yolks from whites. Reserve whites to fill with deviled mixture.

Thorolastic
WARNING
AVISO

Fancy Chicken Salad

SERVES 2

One of the hardest things to do when making a restaurant menu is to come up with a clever name for everything. With this salad, there's nothing really clever to it. It has pears, figs, spicy walnuts, a really nice blue cheese, and a Champagne Vinaigrette. All of those items seemed sort of fancy to us—certainly more so than your average side salad of iceberg lettuce with tomatoes and carrots. So we just named it something pretty simple: Fancy Chicken Salad. It's one of the most popular salads on the menu.

CHAMPAGNE VINAIGRETTE (MAKES APPROXIMATELY 6 CUPS)

INGREDIENTS	MEASURE	CUT	PREPARATION
Shallots	1/4 cup	Rough chopped	(1) In deep mixing bowl, use electric mixer to combine first 5 ingredients.
Champagne vinegar	1 cup		
Kosher salt	1 teaspoon		
White pepper	3 teaspoons		
Basil, fresh	1/2 cup	Chopped	
Olive oil	4 cups		(2) Slowly add oil while mixing to emusify and create thick mixture. (3) Store in large mason jar in refrigerator.

SPICY WALNUTS (MAKES 2 CUPS)

INGREDIENTS	MEASURE	CUT	PREPARATION
Walnut halves	2 cups		(1) Preheat convection oven to 350 degrees. (2) In large stainless-steel bowl, combine all ingredients well. (3) Place walnuts on sheet pan in oven for 15 minutes, stirring every 5 minutes. (4) Allow to cool at room temperature, place in colander and shake off excess seasonings, and store in airtight container.
Brown sugar	1/2 cup		
Cayenne pepper	2 tablespoons		
Sesame oil	2 tablespoons		

FIGS I learned something about figs recently. I just always assumed you had to wait to harvest them until the fruit turned from green to brown, but not all varieties do that. There's one kind we get at the restaurant that is bright green and looks too early to be ripe, but when you cut it open, it's as bright as a strawberry and even sweeter to eat. The goal is to pick them when they're easy to pinch.

We have figs year-round on our Fancy Chicken Salad, and we use them in our Round Rock Bee Keeper cocktail with whiskey and Round Rock honey. I also love to use them with jalapeños to make jam. We mainly source our figs from Lightsey Farms in Mexia, but when the season is near its end, I take them from anyone who's willing to bring them to me.

ACHIOTE CHICKEN BREAST (MAKES 6-8 BONELESS CHICKEN BREASTS)

INGREDIENTS	MEASURE	CUT		PREPARATION
Achiote paste	1 ounce		**On prepared grill, cook 2 minutes per side, flipping twice per side.*	(1) In mixing bowl, combine achiote with all ingredients except chicken.
Orange juice	½ cup			
White vinegar	½ cup			
Black pepper	1 teaspoon			
All spice	½ teaspoon	Ground		
Garlic cloves	2 tablespoons	Chopped		
Paprika	½ tablespoon			
Kosher salt	½ tablespoon			
Oregano	½ tablespoon	Ground		
Chicken breasts, boneless	6 to 8			(2) Marinate chicken in bowl, covered in refrigerator, up to 12 hours.

COMPOSED SALAD (MAKES 2 SERVINGS)

INGREDIENTS	MEASURE	CUT		PREPARATION
Achiote chicken breast	6-ounce breast	Diced	**After cooking chicken, slice in 4 pieces, then chop 3 more times for 12 total dice.*	(1) In large stainless-steel bowl using tongs, combine chicken, greens, vinaigrette, and pears, and toss well.
Iceberg	2 ounces	Shredded		
Spring mix	2 ounces			
Champagne Vinaigrette	2 ounces			
Pears	2 ounces	Sliced		
Blue cheese	¼ cup	Crumbled		(2) Place salad on plates; top with cheese, walnuts, and figs; and season to taste.
Spiced Walnuts	2 tablespoons			
Figs	¼ cup	Sliced		
Black pepper	To taste	Fresh milled		

ACHIOTE is a spice blend or a paste that we use for pork, fish, and chicken dishes. The main component is the red annatto seed, which gives the dish bright color. Annatto is a traditional Mexican ingredient for the Yucatan region, used for pibil, for example, and it gives pork pibil its reddish color. When you add orange juice to it and a bit of vinegar, it gets more vibrantly red, almost like a blood orange. Achiote/annatto has a mild flavor that gets a bump from OJ, and vice versa. If you marinade chicken in just OJ, it tastes good, but it doesn't look that great. So we add the achiote to give it color.

Fancy Chicken Salad

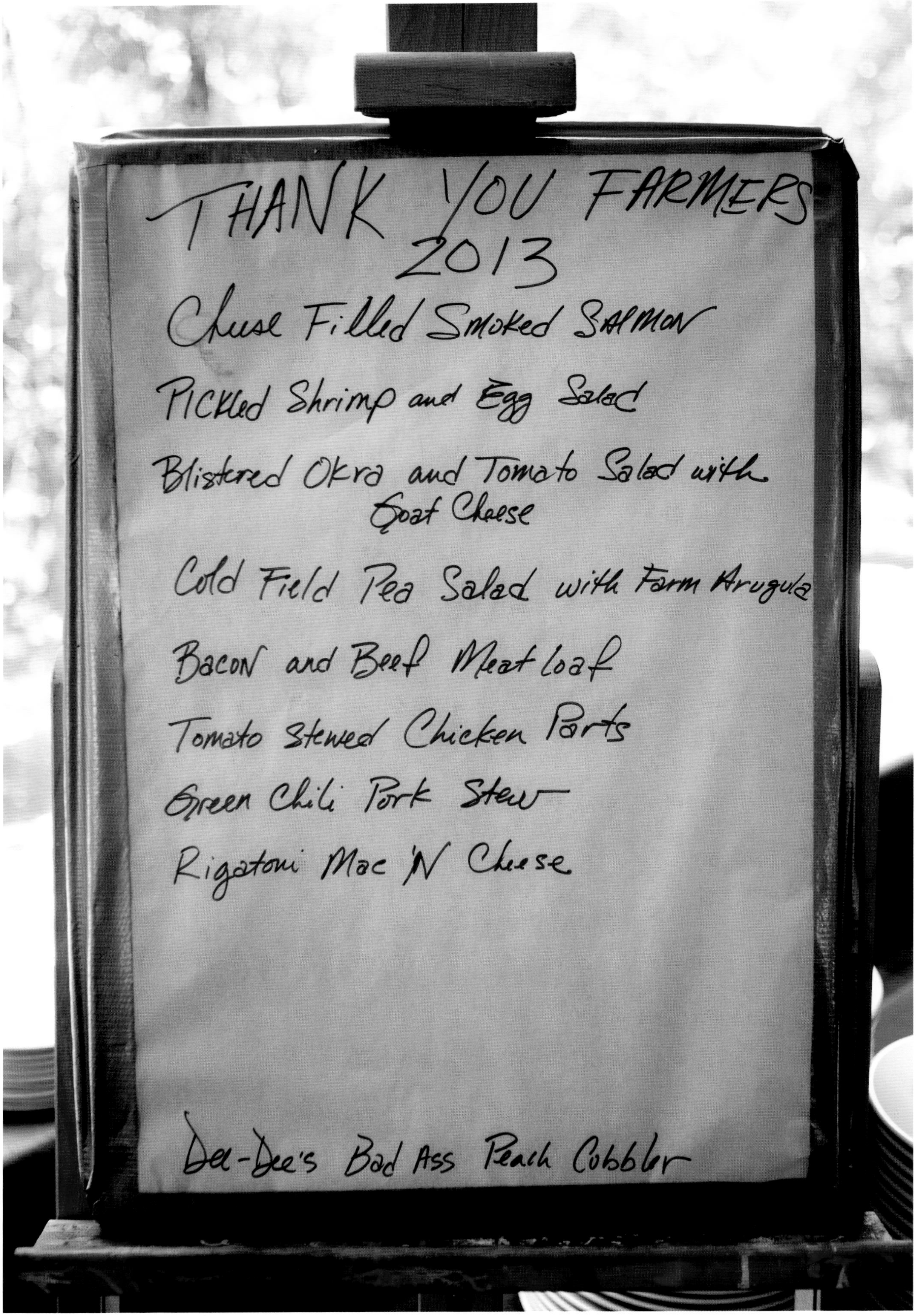
THANK YOU FARMERS
2013
Cheese Filled Smoked Salmon
Pickled Shrimp and Egg Salad
Blistered Okra and Tomato Salad with Goat Cheese
Cold Field Pea Salad with Farm Arugula
Bacon and Beef Meatloaf
Tomato Stewed Chicken Parts
Green Chili Pork Stew
Rigatoni Mac 'N Cheese
Dee-Dee's Bad Ass Peach Cobbler

Farmers Appreciation Lunch

At the close of each summer, my son Bryce collaborates with us to host a Saturday afternoon Farmers Appreciation Lunch. We do it for a simple reason: We believe in taking care of the people who take care of us. When we need certain types of food, these people always provide. Every day they wake up and deal with whatever Mother Nature throws their way, so throwing them a party is the very least we can do to thank them.

Together, Bryce and I work with our chefs and staff on a big menu that shows off the beautiful fruits, vegetables, meats, and cheeses they produce for us. We serve a family-style buffet at Jack Allen's as a late lunch after the farmers have packed up from farmers markets around Austin. It gives them a chance to relax with their families, catch up with other farmers and purveyors, eat some good home-style food, and enjoy a beer or a margarita—or both!

When we first started doing this, after Jack Allen's opened, we hosted maybe 30 people inside the restaurant. But now we're welcoming on our patio nearly 150 people from about 40 area farms.

It's an important event for everyone at the restaurant and something Tom and I are both committed to. It's about breaking bread and having community. It makes us stop our busy schedules and focus on the whole reason we run our restaurants the way we do, which is to support our farming community. It's about giving thanks, walking the walk, and staying true to the philosophy we tout on our menus.

These farmers and purveyors work so hard and rarely have time to sit together and celebrate. It's a great joy to serve them and savor the summer's best ingredients.

Cured Salmon
(see page 29)

DulceVida

JACK ALLEN'S
KITCHEN
Diana "DeeDee" Sanchez
Pastry Chef

Heirloom Caprese Salad

SERVES 4

When we get lucky, heirloom tomatoes can be the best thing you've ever put in your mouth. But they aren't always really pretty. So we came up with a way to serve them that honors the wonderful flavor and makes a pretty presentation too. We cut up the tomatoes and add good olive oil, herbs, and some good goat cheese. You can use any number of cheeses, but I like the herbaceous quality goat cheese brings to the salad. Using the mason jars is also a great way to manage portion control, plus everyone gets their own little salad.

INGREDIENTS	MEASURE	CUT		PREPARATION
Heirloom tomatoes, multiple colors	1 pound	Sliced and randomly cut		(1) Place one layer of tomatoes in 8-ounce mason jars.
Red onion	4 tablespoons	Chopped		(2) Place 1 tablespoon of onion on top of tomatoes and continue layers in alternating colors to fill jars.
Basil leaves	16			(3) Place 4 basil leaves on top of tomatoes in each jar.
Olive oil Champagne vinegar	¾ cup ¼ cup		**We like Texas Olive Ranch.*	(4) Mix oil and vinegar, and fill each jar to top.
Salt and pepper	To taste			(5) Sprinkle seasonings on top and seal jars tightly. Refrigerate until ready to use, no more than 2 hours.
Fresh goat cheese	8 ounces	Crumbled	**We like Swede Farm Goat Cheese.*	(6) Divide cheese crumbles onto 4 plates evenly. Shake mason jars to combine ingredients and pour 1 jar onto goat cheese on each plate.

Fried Green Tomatoes with Corn Salad

Not only is this a Southern dish that fits our restaurant's flavor profile, but we can get green tomatoes pretty much throughout the year. Farmers sell them when they can't get the really sweet ripe tomatoes. Even when tomatoes get going in summer, farmers need to thin the crop, so they cut green ones early. Our Fried Green Tomatoes are a little bit different. In the South you see them breaded with cornmeal and fried in bacon fat, which makes them gritty, in my opinion. Instead, we use Parmesan and Panko breadcrumbs to get a nice crispness. They are good on sliders, and we also love to serve them with a dollop of fresh Gulf crab.

FRIED GREEN TOMATOES (SERVES 3-4)

INGREDIENTS	MEASURE	CUT		PREPARATION
Buttermilk Eggs	2 cups 2			(1) For buttermilk wash, in bowl whisk together buttermilk and eggs.
Parmesan cheese Panko breadcrumbs	1 cup 2 cups	Grated		(2) For breading mixture, in bowl combine cheese and breadcrumbs.
Green tomatoes Seasoned Flour *(see page 191)*	3 2 cups	Sliced ¼-inch thick	**Fry in 2 or 3 batches so as not to crowd.*	(3) Prepare electric fryer or stovetop fryer to 350 degrees. (4) Holding edge, toss tomatoes in Seasoned Flour. (5) Place tomatoes in buttermilk wash one at a time. (6) Dredge in breading mixture and press to coat well. (7) Place in fryer; shake after 30 seconds so tomatoes do not stick together. (8) Fry approximately 1 ½ minutes per side until crispy and golden brown. (9) Lift basket and drain. (10) Serve topped with Corn Salad.

CORN SALAD (MAKES: ENOUGH FOR 16 FRIED GREEN TOMATOES)

INGREDIENTS	MEASURE	CUT	PREPARATION
Corn, sweet	1 cup	Roasted and cut from cob	(1) In large mixing bowl, combine all ingredients and mix well.
Sweet and Spicy Avocado Sauce *(see page 54)*	½ cup		(2) Serve on Fried Green Tomatoes.
Arugula	1 cup		
Red bell pepper	¼ cup	¼-inch diced	
Red onion	¼ cup	¼-inch diced	
Gulf crab meat	1 cup		
Salt and pepper	To taste		

Okra Tomato Salad

SERVES 6

Okra is a good sign of the season. I like using it, but I always go for the baby okra—it's not as full of that gelatinous stuff. We cut them lengthwise and roast them in the broiler to dry them out a bit. It adds an earthy grilled flavor. And then we add a nice summer tomato and some quality olive oil. You can use any feta for this salad, but we like the goat feta from Swede Farms. It's crumbly and rich and has a nice bite to it.

INGREDIENTS	MEASURE	CUT	PREPARATION
Okra	3⁄4 pounds	Sliced in half lengthwise after roasting	(1) Preheat oven to broil. (2) Toss together okra, oil, and seasonings, place on sheet pan, and roast until skin blisters.
Olive oil	3 tablespoons		
Salt and pepper	To taste		
Onion	1 medium	Chopped fine	(3) Mix onion with next 4 ingredients, and add okra, combining well.
Red wine vinegar	2 teaspoons		
Dijon mustard	1 tablespoon		
Kosher salt	1 teaspoon		
Black pepper	1 teaspoon		
Tomatoes	5	Cut into wedges	(4) Toss tomatoes, cheese, and olive oil with okra mixture, and get your fork on.
Feta cheese	1⁄2 pound		
Olive oil	1⁄2 cup		

OKRA is one of those things that you either love or hate. Most people grew up having to eat slimy boiled okra, but you can cook it to make it great, and you can simply pickle it. Okra makes a perfect garnish for a good martini. Or dust them with a little cornmeal and flour, fry them up, and pop them in your mouth. We also make gumbo using okra, but I've learned over the years that okra in gumbo is sacrilege to some people, whereas others really love it. Either way, we make it clear on the menu if there's okra in the gumbo or not.

Honestly, my favorite way to use okra is to grill them and then stew them. The perfect okra is 1½ to 2 inches long or they are too big and mealy. Grilling does two things. First, the gelatinous substance on the inside steams out but they stay tender. Second, that smoky flavor enhances a good mix of tomatoes, corn, peppers, and onions. Use a grilling basket so your okra doesn't fall through the grates.

Summer Squash
Casserole
Fresh Hull Pea Ragout

Green Bean and Red Potato Casserole

Junkplant (Eggplant) Casserole

Summer Squash Casserole

SERVES 6

I love casseroles for a lot of reasons, but really they are the best way to use up what's in season in a flavorful way. It's certainly better than boiling. A lot of people grew up with boiled squash, but that is just boring. Roasting and baking brings out good flavors in just about any vegetable. This recipe is pretty simple to showcase the squash itself, but you can easily add a gratin for another level of flavor and texture.

INGREDIENTS	MEASURE	CUT		PREPARATION
Squash/zucchini	1 pound		**Mix the variety if you like.*	(1) Preheat oven to 350 degrees. (2) In heavy cast-iron or porcelain casserole pot, sauté first 5 ingredients slowly for approximately 5 minutes, and season to taste. (3) Bake for approximately 20 minutes.
Butter	1/4 pound	Cut in 3/4-inch slices		
Tomatoes	2	Chopped		
Onion	1 medium	Chopped fine		
Garlic	2 tablespoons	Chopped		
Salt and pepper	To taste			

Fresh Hull Pea Ragout

SERVES 6

This is basically a mix of field peas. You have hulled peas—creamers, black-eyeds, and purple. If you have only one of them, that's fine, but I like the mix, fresh ones rather than dry. Just know that fresh peas cook quicker. The fresh corn, onions, and basil add to the ragout for more texture. This ragout serves great with steak or pork chops. Give it an extra kick with a little homemade Chile Purée Sauce *(see page 112)*.

INGREDIENTS	MEASURE	CUT		PREPARATION
Fresh hull peas	6 cups			(1) In soup pot, cook peas and bacon, covered with water, on medium heat until tender, 30 to 40 minutes.
Bacon	12 pieces	Chopped		
Black pepper	1 tablespoon			(2) Add next 6 ingredients, and simmer for 15 minutes.
Beef broth (boxed is fine)	3 cups			
Sage	4 tablespoons	Chopped		
Basil	4 tablespoons	Chopped		
Corn, fresh	2 cups			
Red onion	2 cups	Chopped		
Butter	1/4 pound		**Add your favorite cheese on top.*	(3) Stir in butter and seasonings, and enjoy.
Salt and pepper	To taste			

Junkplant (Eggplant) Casserole

SERVES 6

It's no secret that I'm not a fan of the eggplant. It tastes like a sponge. It looks like a sponge. And it has a lot of water in it, just like a sponge. It's also a gray mess when you serve it by itself. To save it, I put it in a casserole dish with pretty tomatoes and red onion and let the flavors cook together in the oven. If you work with the smaller eggplant, I suggest not peeling it. The skin is not as tough as on the big eggplant, and leaving it on just looks better.

INGREDIENTS	MEASURE	CUT	PREPARATION
Eggplant	1 pound	Cut in 2-inch cubes	(1) In heavy cast-iron or porcelain casserole pot on medium heat, sauté all ingredients slowly for approximately 30 minutes, until tender.
Olive oil	4 tablespoons		
Tomatoes	2	Chopped	
Red onion	1 medium	Chopped fine	
Garlic	2 tablespoons	Chopped	
Salt and pepper	To taste		(2) Season to taste.
Lime	½ for juice		(3) Squeeze lime over casserole, and serve.

Green Bean and Red Potato Casserole

SERVES 6

People always ask me about my favorite foods. I have a lot of favorites, but this is on top of my list. Take a really good sweet green bean, a good fresh potato, and sour cream, and it's unbelievable. What sets it off is when you add a few dashes of our homemade Chile Purée Sauce *(see page 112)*. The combination has great texture, creaminess, and a little bit of heat, all in one. It's the best.

INGREDIENTS	MEASURE	CUT	PREPARATION
Green beans, freshly picked	1 pound		(1) In large pot of water, bring beans and potatoes to boil and simmer approximately 30 minutes, until tender.
Red potatoes	1 pound, small	Quartered	
Sour cream	1 cup		(2) Drain, transfer to large bowl, fold in sour cream and vinegar, and season.
Vinegar, your favorite kind	2 tablespoons		
Salt and pepper	To taste		

Tomato Basil Pie

SERVES 6-8

There's just something about tomato pie. It's Southern, it's comforting, and it's a great way to use up all the tomatoes that may grow in your backyard in summer. It's like an upside-down quiche. Plus it's really simple. Just tomatoes, basil, cheese, and a little mayonnaise. You really can't screw it up. And this is an occasion when it's completely okay to use a store-bought piecrust.

INGREDIENTS	MEASURE	CUT		PREPARATION
Tomatoes, ripe Salt and pepper	3 To taste	Sliced thin		(1) Lightly season slices and allow to drain on paper towel. (2) Preheat oven to 300 degrees.
Cheddar cheese Monterey Jack cheese Parmesan cheese	½ cup ½ cup ½ cup	Grated Grated Grated		(3) Combine cheddar with other cheeses in small bowl.
Prepared pie shell	1			(4) Layer tomatoes in pie shell.
Basil leaves	6	Broken into pieces with fingertips		(5) Place basil pieces on tomatoes. (6) Sprinkle cheese mixture on top.
Eggs Mayonnaise	2 1 cup		**What would Jack do? I like the crust on top, so by all means cool down the pie for 10 minutes, put a serving platter on top, and flip it over. Boom! Crust on top.*	(7) Whisk together eggs and mayonnaise in small bowl, and pour evenly over pie ingredients. (8) Bake for approximately 45 minutes, until golden brown and bubbly.

*TIP Be sure to draw out the water from the tomatoes by letting them sit salted and peppered for a while. For the recipe, we ask you to drain on a paper towel. But you can drain them in a bowl and reserve the water for a really good Bloody Mary.

RICHARDSON FARMS

AS TOLD BY JIM RICHARDSON

I DON'T KNOW if there was ever really one time in my life when I decided to work with animals or start a farm. It is just something I think I was always meant to do. I grew up in Cooke County in north Central Texas. My grandfather was a farmer, as was his father. When I was a kid, I spent most of my free time out on the farm with my grandfather. I went to stay with him and my grandmother on weekends, holidays, and most of the summers. He taught me to love the land and produce crops; how to love animals and treat them correctly. I don't think there is a greater lesson he could have taught me.

When I went to college, I knew I liked working with animals and agriculture, so I went into a profession in which I could contribute to the welfare of animals. For 41 years, my passion was veterinary medicine. For a number of years I was a partner in a mixed-animal practice in north Central Texas, treating everything from cows and horses to pigs, chickens, cats, and dogs. Later, I moved to the Austin area and ran a small practice for dogs, cats, and other house pets. All during that time, I leased a little land to have a family farm. My wife, Kay, my sons, Mike and Lance, and I grew watermelon, tomatoes, cantaloupes, peaches, and apples. I did my day job and then worked on the farm in the evenings and over the weekend. Kay is from Nebraska and didn't grow up in farming, but I have managed to drag her along with me over the years and she has grown to love it.

Once we had settled in Austin, I felt a real yearning to have a farm of my own. In 2000, we found a place to buy. It had a little farmhouse that we rejuvenated so that we could stay in it on weekends. We did traditional row crops, like corn and wheat, and eventually joined a Community Supported Agriculture (CSA) program. Once we really got going, we started selling our vegetables, eggs, and tomatoes, and anything else we could grow, at area farmers markets. Eventually, I added grass-fed beef into the mix.

By 2007, we realized we really wanted to focus on animals. They have always been my love. So we phased out our vegetables and transitioned to growing pigs along with beef, chickens, and turkeys.

We met most of our customers from our stand at the farmers market, including a lot of chefs. But it didn't take long before we started getting orders direct. Carl Leaf of Kerbey Lane was one of our first customers, and eventually others came—like James Holmes of Olivia, Jesse Griffiths of Dai Due, and Bryce Gilmore of Barley Swine and Odd Duck—which is how we eventually met Jack Gilmore.

Because of my background as a veterinarian, a lot of people ask if I treat the animals that get sick. If we have an animal that gets sick, I'll manage it if it requires therapy, but I make sure those animals don't go into the food chain to our customers. Honestly, if you don't stress the animals, they don't get sick like you see at feedlots and factory farms. When you push them hard, they break with disease.

We also control a lot of what the animals eat because we grow their food on our farm. We have everything from wheat, corn, barley, and alfalfa to an array of green salad crops like turnips, mustard greens, kale, and other cold weather crops. That allows us to have green foods on the land for them at all times. Altogether we work with about 300 pigs, 700 egg-laying chickens, 1,000 broiler chickens, 1,000 turkeys, and 70 head of cattle, though all of those numbers vary a bit throughout the year.

MY SON MIKE and step-grandson, Conner, also work with me, and we have another generation beyond that that hopefully will make this farm live on after me. It has been so rewarding to see that passion pass on through my family. After all, it is hard work. Most days we are up at around 4:30, feeding and watering, checking fences and making sure the animals are secure. Add to that the deliveries we make directly to restaurants and farmers markets on weekends. It's all about staying organized.

I love being out on the farm but also out there telling people about what we do. I love bringing people out here to see how it all works. This is what I call "the new old way." We are learning about the mistakes the industry has made over the past few decades and finding ways to go back to the old way of doing things. The result is that we are starting to have cleaner, better foods. If I can help educate people about the immeasurable value in what we can do for our local food economy, then I feel like I have done the job I was put on this earth to do.

PHOTO BY SARAH TEVELDAL

Grilled Thick-Cut Pork Chop with Redneck Chimichurri

SERVES 2

This was a dish I made up while we were on a photo shoot for this book. We already had these great thick-cut chops from Richardson Farms when we went to Broken Arrow Ranch one day. I had brought along a molcajete to use as a prop, but we ended up mashing up a bunch of green onion, jalapeño, cilantro, and garlic with some olive oil, salt, and pepper. It looked so good, we had to pour it over the pork chops we'd just grilled on the fire.

INGREDIENTS	MEASURE	CUT		PREPARATION
Pork chops Kosher salt and cracked black pepper	2			(1) Prepare grill. (2) Season both sides of chops and grill to 135 degrees in thickest part of meat, 2 to 3 minutes per side, flipping twice per side. (3) Serve with Redneck Chimichurri *(below)*.

REDNECK CHIMICHURRI (MAKES 3 CUPS)

INGREDIENTS	MEASURE	CUT		PREPARATION
Garlic Onion	3 to 6 cloves 2 tablespoons	 Chopped		(1) In food processor, pulse garlic and onion until finely chopped.
Cilantro, fresh Jalapeño, fresh	2 cups, firmly packed ¼ cup	 Diced		(2) Add cilantro and jalapeños, and pulse briefly until finely chopped.
Olive oil Red wine vinegar Lime juice Kosher salt and cracked black pepper	½ cup 2 tablespoons 1 tablespoon To taste		**Chimichurri lasts in the refrigerator up to 3 weeks.*	(3) Transfer mixture to bowl to retain texture, and stir in oil, vinegar, and juice; season to taste.

11
812/0

810/0
816/0
795/0

Grilled Skirt Steak

SERVES 6

At both Jack Allen's restaurants, we have the capability to add wood to our grill, and we'll cook skirt steak with all different sorts of wood, from pecan to fig or peach wood. From there, we pretty much make kind of a street taco type of thing out of it. My favorite thing to do is to put it on queso flameado, in which we melt really good Monterey Jack cheese with some green chiles. We add the steak on top, so you can build your own cheesy taco.

INGREDIENTS	MEASURE	CUT	PREPARATION
Lemons	2	Cut and juiced	(1) Combine first 5 ingredients, and marinate steak for 4 hours.
Limes	2	Cut and juiced	
Garlic	2 cloves	Chopped	
Soy sauce	2 tablespoons		
Worchestershire sauce	1 tablespoon		
Skirt steak	2 pounds	Trimmed	(2) Prepare grill to high heat. (3) Grill steak 4 to 5 minutes per side or to perferred doneness. (4) Let rest on cutting board for 5 minutes, then cut across the grain into ½-inch slices. (5) Serve with tortillas, pico de gallo, guacamole, and shredded cheese.

SKIRT STEAK In Central Texas, skirt steak is really a staple item. The bad thing is that there is only so much skirt in one cow and it is so overused that it is hard to come by. In the past 20 years, fajitas have really taken off. If you go to a Mexican food restaurant, you don't even get skirt steak anymore. You get flank or you get something else but it is not skirt, I promise you that. But 30 years ago, you couldn't even find skirt steak in a Chicago or Charleston restaurant because they put it into ground beef.

Skirt steak has such a great flavor and texture to it. If you marinate it, cook it, and cut it right—"cut" being the operative word—it's the best meat you will eat. You have to cut it across the grain. If you don't cut it right, it's going to be the chewiest meat you will eat.

Head-to-Tail Shrimp

SERVES 6

This is something I served when I competed at the Great American Seafood Cook Off in New Orleans. And this recipe put us in third place out of 50 states. We applied the popular nose-to-tail culinary philosophy, using the whole shrimp to make a meatball. Then we made really thin strands of zucchini to be like pasta and a nice savory Tomato Jam to go along with it.

TOMATO JAM

INGREDIENTS	MEASURE	CUT	PREPARATION
Olive oil	1/3 cup		(1) In saucepan, combine all ingredients and boil for 1 minute. (2) Purée with immersion blender, and cool rapidly in ice bath.
Garlic	2 cloves	Minced	
Red tomatoes	1 cup	Diced	
Honey	1/4 cup		
Red pepper flakes	1/2 tablespoon		

ZUCCHINI NOODLES

INGREDIENTS	MEASURE	CUT	PREPARATION
Zucchini	2	Shaved to thin noodles with mandolin	(1) Right before serving, lightly dress noodles with oil and season to taste.
Olive oil	To taste		
Salt and pepper	To taste		

HEAD-TO-TAIL GULF SHRIMP MEATBALLS

INGREDIENTS	MEASURE	CUT	PREPARATION
Shrimp, shelled	1 pound	Deveined and chopped fine	(1) In large bowl, combine all ingredients and mix well. (2) Form 3/4-inch meatballs (approximately 20) and stage for frying.
Eggs, raw	2		
Chives	1/4 cup	Chopped	
Jalapeños	1 tablespoon	Seeded and minced	
Panko breadcrumbs	3 tablespoons		
Kosher salt	1/2 teaspoon		
Pepper, freshly ground	1/2 teaspoon		
Vegetable oil	For frying	**To serve, dollop Tomato Jam on appetizer plate, add small portion of Zucchini Noodles, and place 3 Shrimp Meatballs in the center.*	(3) In large cast-iron skillet, heat 2 inches oil to 350 degrees. (4) Fry meatballs for approximately 3 minutes, stirring occasionally, until cooked, and drain on paper towels.

LIGHTSEY FARMS

ON MOST MORNINGS, Mary Lightsey climbs into her truck and drives the property to see what needs to be harvested. As she makes her rounds, she also thinks about what needs to be planted in the near future.

"It's a constant cycle," says Mary. "When we're not in a drought year, we plant somewhere around 1,000 new trees each year, but it's often more."

For nearly a century, Mary's family has farmed approximately 100 acres outside the small Texas town of Mexia, 40 miles east of Waco. It is a tight-knit community of families, rural ranchers, and farmers. Eric Elijah Lightsey homesteaded the property in 1918. His son, Eric Ellice, was born there in the 1920s and eventually took over the land. Here, he raised two daughters, Mary and Lisa, who grew up working the land with their father and learning about planting and harvesting seasons. They also learned to love the soil their family had cultivated.

The farm became known for its diverse array of fruit crops, from peaches, figs, and pomegranates to apricots, plums, and nectarines. But each season also included a small variety of vegetables, like field peas and sweet potatoes. Working on the farm not only taught the girls a healthy respect for land and family but also gave them a sense of ownership in the heritage of the farm. And it paid their way through college, which led both Mary and Lisa to begin careers as teachers.

But when their father passed away, in 2009, the sisters had to make some tough decisions.

"We had mountains of fruit trees we had been growing on for three generations," says Mary. "It was important to us not to lose it all."

For a short time, the sisters left their careers in education to keep the family farm alive.

"At first, we thought we could alternate years, with one of us teaching one year and the other working the farm," says Mary. "But as we got into it, Lisa realized she really wanted to be in the classroom. So I do most of the farm work, and she helps out when she can."

Depending on the type of tree, the farm can expect an average age of 25 years, which keeps Mary regularly assessing the best way to keep her crops moving forward.

Spring and summer are busiest. Fruit is at its peak and Mary works endless hours to harvest it for markets and wholesalers. Her produce goes to Whole Foods Market in Austin as well as a number of farmers markets throughout the state, from Dallas to Houston. That means she is often on the road, making weekly deliveries.

"A big part of what we do is manage our relationships with the people we grow for," says Mary. "I really enjoy getting out to the markets and socializing. I put a lot of hours into the farm and a lot in the brutal Texas heat, but getting out to talk with the people who enjoy the produce is the most rewarding part."

Mary Lightsey and Lisa Lightsey Hadden are third-generation farmers, continuing what their grandfather began in 1918.

Goat Cheese Peach or Fig Tart

SERVES 8-10

This dessert is a perfect blank canvas for just about any fruit that's in season. For summertime, it's figs or peaches, but you can make it with apples, pears, or plums too. I like using goat cheese for a nice savory component. This is a simple tart, and it always comes out beautifully. It's a real showstopper when you're entertaining guests.

INGREDIENTS	MEASURE	CUT	PREPARATION
Graham cracker crumbs	2 cups		(1) Preheat oven to 350 degrees. (2) For crust, combine first 4 ingredients in medium-sized bowl, then press into bottom of greased 9-inch springform pan. (3) Bake for 5 minutes, and set aside while preparing filling.
Sugar	2 tablespoons		
Pecans	¼ cup	Finely chopped	
Butter	¼ cup	Melted	
Cream cheese, softened	12 ounces		(4) In small deep bowl, beat cheeses with mixer until smooth, about 5 minutes.
Goat cheese	4 ounces		
Sugar	4 ounces		(5) Add sugar and beat another 2 minutes.
Eggs	2		(6) Add eggs, mix well, and pour into prepared crust.
Figs, fresh	1 pint	Sliced	(7) Arrange fruit (peaches, figs, or both) on top of tart, leaving no spaces between (fruit will spread during baking).
Peaches or figs	4	Peeled and cut into wedges	
Sugar	1 tablespoon		(8) Sprinkle sugar over fruit, cover tart with foil, and bake for 30 minutes. (9) Uncover and bake for 15 to 20 minutes more, until center is set. (10) Refrigerate in pan at least 4 hours before removing, slicing, and serving.

Blondie Brownie Pie

SERVES 6-8

This is our take on a classic Tollhouse cookie pie. We use really good white chocolate and a nice rich filling and bake it off with walnuts in a piecrust. We serve it warm with Amy's Mexican Vanilla ice cream and also a caramel sauce we make from the filling. You can add just about anything you want to the filling, like chocolate chips or pecans. And if you want a boozy flavor, switch out the vanilla for bourbon. It's delicious.

INGREDIENTS	MEASURE	CUT	PREPARATION
Eggs	2, plus 1 for egg wash		(1) Preheat oven to 325 degrees. (2) Mix pie ingredients in mixer until just combined. (3) Whisk 1 egg with 1 tablespoon water for egg wash.
Flour	½ cup		
Sugar	½ cup		
Brown sugar	½ cup		
Butter, melted	1 cup		
White chocolate	1 cup	Chopped	
Walnuts	½ cup	Chopped	
Mexican vanilla	1 tablespoon		
Piecrust, store bought is fine	1 9-inch		(4) Pour pie mixture into piecrust, brush edges with egg wash, and bake for 55 minutes, turning pie midway for even baking.

Jams and Jellies

I use these words—jams and jellies—interchangeably because the terms don't really matter, but there's nothing insignificant about having a good supply of them around the kitchen. We use them in so many ways, and I'm not talking about breakfast toast. With all the seasonal flavors throughout the year, we use jams and jellies for glazes on steaks and other grilled meats, as bases for tarts and other desserts, in cocktails, or as finishing sauces for any number of dishes. Make the most of the seasonal ingredients you have. We may get a lot of produce that we can't use fast enough before it spoils. This is our way of preserving the bounty for later use and avoiding waste.

Plum Jam

MAKES 6-8 8-OUNCE JARS

INGREDIENTS	MEASURE	CUT	PREPARATION
Plums Water	3 ½ pounds 3 cups	Peeled, cored, diced	(1) Place plums in large pot covered with water, bring to boil, reduce heat, cover, and simmer until plums are tender, approximately 5 minutes. (2) Crush cooked plums with whisk and simmer 5 more minutes. (3) Strain until all liquid is drained.
Sugar	7 ½ cups		(4) In saucepan, mix sugar and plums, and simmer for 20 minutes.
Butter	1 teaspoon		(5) Melt in butter and mix well.
Fruit pectin, powdered	2 ounces		(6) Stir in pectin thoroughly and boil for 1 minute, stirring constantly. (7) Cool in refrigerator, seal in jars, and refrigerate (use within 30 days).

Prickly Pear Jam

MAKES 6–8 8-OUNCE JARS

INGREDIENTS	MEASURE	CUT	PREPARATION
Prickly pears Water	3 ½ pounds 4 cups	Washed and cut in half length wise (use gloves because of thorns)	(1) Place prickly pears in large pot covered with water, bring to boil, reduce heat, cover, and simmer until prickly pears are tender, approximately 5 minutes. (2) Crush cooked prickly pears with whisk and cook 5 more minutes. (3) Strain until all liquid is drained. Reserve liquid and discard solids.
Sugar	8 cups		(4) In saucepan mix sugar and liquid, and simmer for 20 minutes.
Lemons	2	Juiced	(5) Stir in juice.
Fruit pectin, powdered	2 ounces		(6) Stir in pectin thoroughly and boil for 1 minute, stirring constantly. (7) Cool in refrigerator, seal in jars, and refrigerate (use within 30 days).

Grilled Jalapeño Jam

MAKES 3–4 8-OUNCE JARS

INGREDIENTS	MEASURE	CUT	PREPARATION
Jalapeños, grilled Sugar White vinegar	12 medium 3 cups 2 tablespoons	Chopped	(1) In saucepot, slowly simmer jalapeños, sugar, and vinegar until softened and thickened, approximately 45 minutes.
Lemons Salt	2 1 teaspoon	Juiced	(2) Using immersion blender, blend in juice and salt. (3) Cool in refrigerator, seal in jars, and refrigerate (use within 30 days).

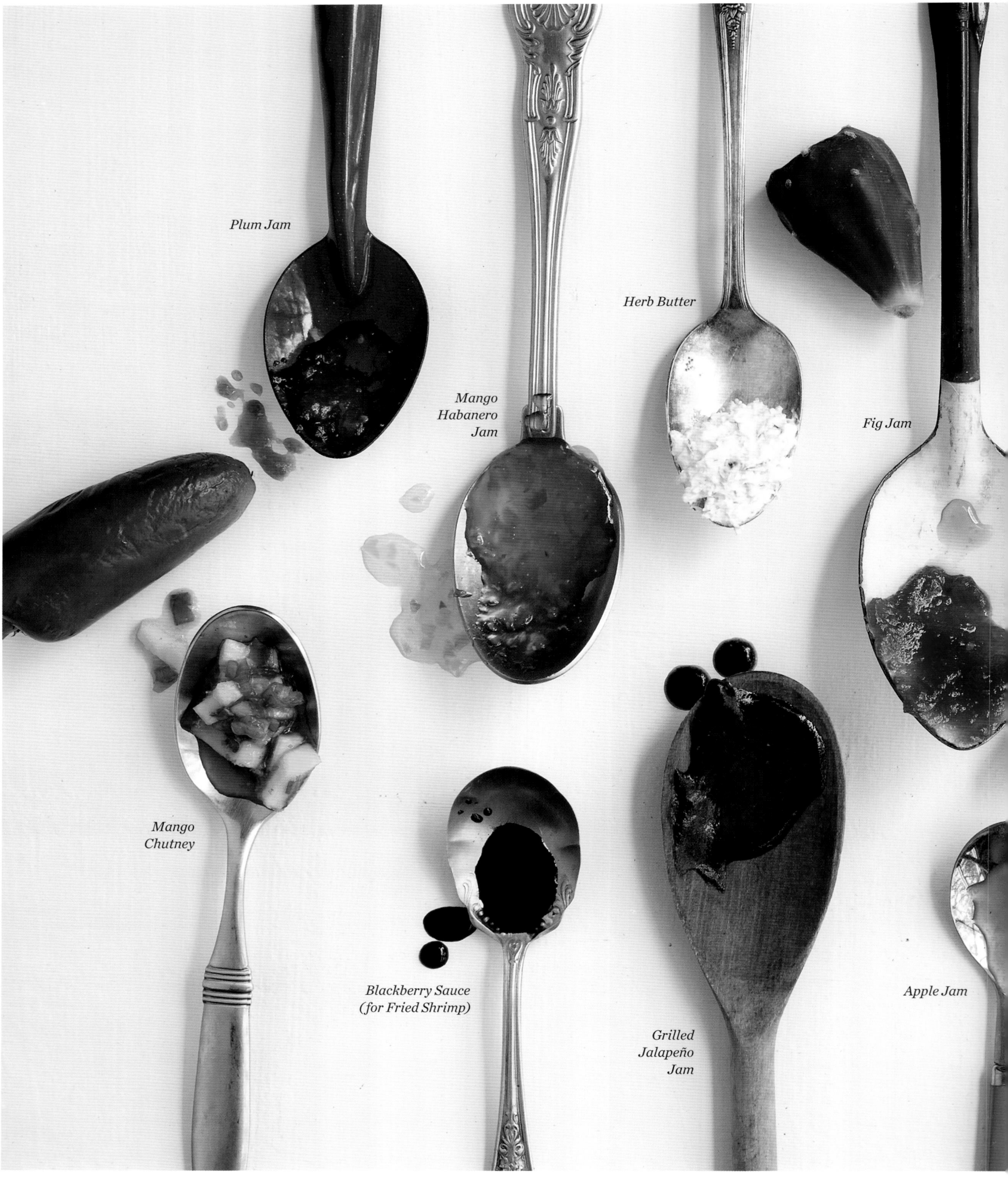
Plum Jam
Herb Butter
Mango
Habanero
Jam
Fig Jam
Mango
Chutney
Blackberry Sauce
(for Fried Shrimp)
Apple Jam
Grilled
Jalapeño
Jam

Pickles

Another way to use seasonal produce without waste: pickling. You can pickle almost anything, preserve it, and honor the work the farmers have done to grow it. The key is to preserve that natural crispness. Pickled ingredients finish off a dish with a little extra burst of flavor and crispy texture.

Pickled Chiles

MAKES 2 32-OUNCE JARS

INGREDIENTS	MEASURE	CUT	PREPARATION
White vinegar Water Pickling spices	1 cup 2 cups ¼ cup	Peeled, cored, diced	(1) In large saucepot, boil first 3 ingredients for 4 to 5 minutes. 2) Strain and reserve liquid.
Chiles (your choice: jalapeño, serrano, habanero, Anaheim)	1 ½ pounds	¼ inch sliced	(3) Boil large pot of water, and blanch chiles for approximately 10 seconds. (4) Divide chiles evenly into jars, fill jars with reserved liquid, secure lids, and pickle for 24 hours until ready to eat.

Pickled Green Beans

MAKES 3-4 32-OUNCE JARS

INGREDIENTS	MEASURE	CUT	PREPARATION
White vinegar Water Pickling spices Dried chiles	1 cup 2 cups ¼ cup 3		(1) In large saucepot, boil first 4 ingredients for 4 to 5 minutes. (2) Strain and reserve liquid.
Green beans	1 pound	Cleaned and stemmed	(3) Place green beans in bowl, pour liquid over them, place plate on top to submerge, and leave at room temperature for 2 to 4 hours. (4) Seal in jars and refrigerate.

Pickled Watermelon Rind

MAKES 2-3 32-OUNCE MASON JARS

INGREDIENTS	MEASURE	CUT	PREPARATION
White vinegar Water Pickling spices Dried chiles Sugar	1 cup 2 cups 1/4 cup 3 2 cups		(1) In large saucepot, boil first 5 ingredients for 4 to 5 minutes. (2) Strain and reserve liquid.
Watermelon rind	1 pound	Outer skin and inside flesh removed; julienned	(3) Place rinds in bowl, pour liquid over them, place plate on top to submerge, and leave at room temperature for 2 to 4 hours. (4) Seal in jars and refrigerate.

Pickled Cucumber

MAKES 2-3 32-OUNCE JARS

INGREDIENTS	MEASURE	CUT	PREPARATION
White vinegar Water Pickling spices Sugar	1 cup 2 cups 1/4 cup 1 cup		(1) In large saucepot, boil first 4 ingredients for 4 to 5 minutes. (2) Strain and reserve liquid.
Cucumbers	1 pound small	Peeled and sliced	(3) Place cucumbers in bowl, pour liquid over them, place plate on top to submerge, and leave at room temperature for 2 to 4 hours. (4) Seal in jars and refrigerate.

LOUNGE

TOM KAMM

AS TOLD BY TOM KAMM

I'M NOT ORIGINALLY from Texas, but I have considered Austin my home for most of my life. I'm from Buffalo, New York, but my family moved here when I was in high school and I stayed to go to the University of Texas for college. I thought I would get a degree in premed to become a physical therapist, but after realizing the amount of chemistry I would have to study, I opted for a marketing degree. Like a lot of people in that stage of life, I worked at a restaurant to help pay my way through school. The only thing is, I never left the business. I liked it too much.

That was in the early 1980s. I waited tables, tended bar, and even did some management, but I mostly enjoyed the Austin lifestyle. I woke up, worked out, rode my bike to Barton Springs to swim, and went to work at night. I worked at interior Mexican cuisine icon Fonda San Miguel for a while, and then I went to Manuel's when it first opened.

I had made a promise to myself that I would own a restaurant by the time I was 30. I was already a general manager at Manuel's, and at just the right time, I had the opportunity to take over about 40 percent of a Round Rock Tex-Mex restaurant called La Margarita. It was losing money and they wanted me to help turn it around. Amazingly enough, I did it. I worked really hard, and the restaurant started making money. I was even able to get the debt paid off. But then they fired me. (When you give someone 40 percent of nothing, it's nothing. But when it becomes something, that's another story.)

I eventually met up with the guys from Z Tejas, Larry Foles and Guy Villavaso. They were opening their Scottsdale location, and I was one of the first managers they hired. I was ready to be a part of something that I could help grow. That's when I met Jack Gilmore. We immediately hit it off, realizing we had a similar way of doing things. After a few years we were committed to the idea that one day we would open our own place. But we were getting a lot from Z Tejas. We were challenged to do new things, and the restaurant company was growing pretty rapidly. It taught me to think quickly and pay attention to what was important.

While I was there, I took over the corporate beverage program and was in charge of the wine, beer, and cocktail menus for all of the restaurants. It was fun because I had my hand in the business side of things as well as the creative side, particularly with developing cocktails.

I MAY NOT BE a master at all things, but I know a little about everything, from what makes a restaurant work financially and how to execute at a high level with food and beverage to hiring and developing staff and fitting all the pieces together to keep it going.

The key is to surround yourself with great people. When you can put together a great staff of people, then you can really think about growing a business.

That's something to which Jack and I stayed true when we planned Jack Allen's Kitchen. We kept things simple. We wanted to create a work environment that our staff could buy into and care about. So instead of a thick corporate manual, we made one simple mission statement for our staff: Be nice. From there, it was about focusing on great food, value, and hospitality.

I remember coming up with the name for the restaurant while on a business trip in Salt Lake City. We were trying to figure out if we were going to call it a "roadhouse" or a "cafe," but nothing seemed quite right. While I was on this trip, I saw a restaurant named Dinah's Kitchen, and it hit me. Jack's Kitchen! It really fit the level of hospitality we wanted to convey; inviting our guests to a meal in Jack's kitchen. We later added his middle name, Allen, to round out the name.

We opened the doors in 2009, right at the beginning of a recession. Everyone thought we were crazy. They were probably right, but we did it anyway. The thing is, we were busy from day one, and we haven't slowed down since.

One thing I hadn't anticipated when opening Jack Allen's was the initial time commitment. I was used to the corporate side of working in restaurants, with no late nights or weekends. So when we opened, it was a bit of a shock. We were 50 years old and suddenly working around the clock. But honestly, I wouldn't change that time for anything. We finally had the restaurant we always wanted.

Working in this industry has been so fulfilling. There was one time early on when I thought I would try something different, and I took a sales job. But the night before I started, I ended up driving myself to the ER with what turned out to be a panic attack. You know you're in the right line of work when you have a panic attack trying to leave it.

When you can put together a great staff of people, then you can really think about growing a business.

Tom Kamm at Riley's Tavern, outside of San Marcos, the first bar to get a liquor license in Texas after Prohibition.

TEXAS
J-A-K
LONE STAR STATE

AUSTIN FOOD & WINE ALLIANCE

BOOTH OPERATOR:
Fire Pit #1
Permit Number: 11121539
Sanitarian
PERMIT TO OPERATE
A
TEMPORARY FOOD
SERVICE
Type of Food: wine
Event Location: 1110 Barton Springs Rd.
This Permit must be posted At the booth.
See reverse side for more info.
Austin/Travis County Health and Human Services Department
Environmental Health Services Division
PO Box 142529
Austin, Texas 78714
Phone: (512) 978-0300 Fax: (512) 978-0322
Date(s) of Operation
Apr 26, 2014 - Apr 27, 2014
Parent RSN 11121420

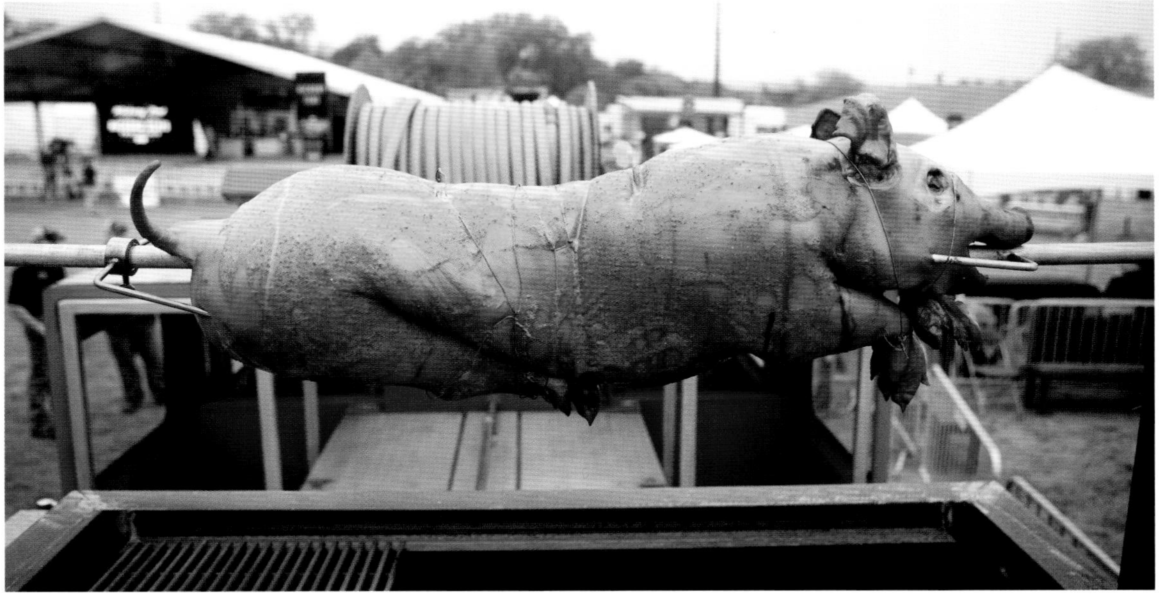

FALL

Gin-Gin Mule

SERVES 1

This is one of my personal favorites of all the drinks we have created. And if you like a Moscow Mule and/or gin, this is right up your alley too. It combines lemon-lime, a dash of sweet, not-your-average-tasting gin and ginger beer, and a salt 'n' peppa rim to give it that kick.

INGREDIENTS	MEASURE	CUT		PREPARATION
Kosher salt Black pepper	2 tablespoons 2 tablespoons	 Coarsely cracked		(1) For salt and pepper rims, combine seasonings in small plate or cocktail rimmer.
Lime	1	Cut into wedges		(2) Rub lime wedge along glass rim, then set glass rim-down in seasoning mixture to coat.
Lime juice, fresh squeezed Lemon juice, fresh squeezed Simple syrup *(see page 18)* Nolet's dry gin	½ ounce ½ ounce ¾ ounce 1 ½ ounces			(3) Fill shaker tin with ice, and add juices, syrup, and gin. (4) Cover shaker tin, shake, and pour into glass.
Ginger beer Mint sprig garnish	2 ounces		**We like Maine Root.* **Make this drink one at a time.*	(5) Top with ginger beer and mint sprig.

Tito's Sage and Grapefruit Splash

Round Rock
Bee Keeper

Tito's Sage and Grapefruit Splash

SERVES 4-6

This one is the Jack Allen's original cocktail, a tasty combo of savory, acidic, sweet, and floral, with a little carbonation. It's easily one of our most popular craft cocktails. And we couldn't have done it without Texas spirit pioneer Tito himself.

INGREDIENTS	MEASURE	CUT		PREPARATION
Sage leaves	16			(1) In 24- to 28-ounce container, stir together sage and syrup. (2) Add a scoop of ice and the next 4 ingredients. (3) Stir and pour into tumblers.
Simple syrup *(see page 18)*	3 ounces			
Lemon	1	Juiced		
Tito's Handmade Vodka	6 ounces			
St-Germaine Elderflower Liqueur	3 ounces			
Rudy Red grapefruit	2 to 3, for 8 ounces juice	Juiced		
Soda water	Splash, or 1 ounce		**We like Fever-Tree.*	(4) Top with splash of soda, and add a straw.

Round Rock Bee Keeper

SERVES 4-6

Around the time we were building the cocktail list, we took a beekeeping class with a bunch of our staff at Round Rock Honey company. We loved the experience so much that we named one of our cocktails after it. We use local Round Rock Honey and add whiskey from a Texas spirits company, Rebecca Creek.

INGREDIENTS	MEASURE	CUT	PREPARATION
Water Round Rock Honey Figs, dried or fresh	32 ounces 8 ounces 1 cup		**For Round Rock Honey–Fig Syrup:** (1) In saucepan boil water and reduce heat, then add honey and figs. (2) Let steep for 15 minutes, and strain out figs; set liquid aside to cool.
Rebecca Creek Texas Spirit Whiskey Luxardo Maraschino Liqueur Round Rock Honey–Fig Syrup Bar Keep Baked Apple Bitters or Apple Bitters	10 ounces 2 ounces 6 ounces 4 to 5 dashes		(3) For cocktail, in small juice carafe add liquors, syrup, and bitters, and stir well.
Figs and apples, for garnish		Sliced and speared	(4) Pour over ice in 9-ounce rocks glass, garnish with speared fruit, and add straw.

Blood Orange Rita

SERVES 4

Blood oranges have amazing flavor and even better color. Every season that I break out this rita, folks keep coming back for more. I do a twist on a traditional margarita with the vibrant blood orange, great locally owned reposado tequila, and Central Market Organics soda. It's easy to execute and one of the restaurant's most talked-about seasonal cocktails.

INGREDIENTS	MEASURE	CUT		PREPARATION
Dulce Vida Reposado Tequila	8 ounces		*Homemade rita mix is a 1-to-1 ratio of lime juice and simple syrup.	(1) In pitcher, combine liquor, juices, rita mix, and soda. (2) Stir and add ice to fill pitcher.
Paula's Texas Orange Liqueur	4 ounces			
Blood orange juice, fresh squeezed	3 ounces			
Orange juice, fresh squeezed	3 ounces			
Homemade rita mix *(see recipe at right)*	6 ounces			
Central Market Organics Blood Orange Soda	6 ounces			
Blood orange peel				(3) Garnish with peel shaving.

REBECCA CREEK
FINE TEXAS
SPIRIT WHISKEY

BALCONES

TEXAS SPIRITS

AS TOLD BY TOM KAMM

To say the Texas spirits industry has exploded in the past few years is an understatement. It's wild. And what's really crazy is Texas spirits aren't just in Texas. We see them when we're traveling all over the country.

Texas distilleries have Tito Beveridge to thank for that. Tito's Handmade Vodka launched in 1997 as the first official distillery in Texas since Prohibition, and to this day, I think it's still one of the best vodkas we produce—even compared to other global brands. The fight to get Texas to license distilleries was long and uphill, but Beveridge was stubborn enough to take it on. His tenacity opened doors for other micro-distilleries, including Paula's Texas Spirits and Treaty Oak Distilling, which took the second and third licenses, respectively, in Texas. Those were the only three licenses for a good 10 years.

Today Texas has more than 50 distilleries either in full operation or with a permit to develop a distillery. That's a huge boom in the past 20 years. Not only is there a new tide of distilleries rolling in around the state, but the quality is there too, particularly with those distilleries that are doing the entire production of their spirits themselves, as what many craft distilleries call grain-to-bottle.

Garrison Brothers Bourbon, out of Hye, is the real deal. Dan Garrison has brought the Kentucky bourbon tradition to Texas, making a smooth spirit that's really good. Noted whiskey enthusiast Jim Murray named Garrison Brothers Cowboy Bourbon the American Micro Whiskey of the Year in his 2014 *Whisky Bible*.

In Austin the relatively new Genius Gin medaled at the fiercely competitive 2014 San Francisco World Wine & Spirits Competition for its Navy Strength gin. Navy Strength is an homage to the early 1800s, when the Royal British Navy required that gin be bottled at 57 percent alcohol by volume. The logic then was that if it was produced at that proof, and somehow it was spilled on gunpowder, said gunpowder could still be fired. Anything with a lower alcohol content would render the ammunition useless.

One other shining star comes from Waco, where Balcones Distilling produces a number of whiskies that have turned heads internationally, giving them a shot beyond gaining a following only in Texas. And in December 2012, a special panel in London invited Balcones to compete against a range of well-known Scottish and Japanese whiskies in what it calls the Best in Glass competition of new international whiskies. Balcones' Single Malt beat all of them as overall Best in Glass against brands such as MacAllen, Balvenie, and GlenMorangie. It was a big awakening for whisky/whiskey aficionados.

In vodka, a recent IRI/Neilson report revealed that both Tito's Vodka and Austin-based Deep Eddy Vodka were in the top 15 in the Texas market. Both are nationally distributed, and Tito's rates as the selected vodka served on United Airlines flights.

We also have some great rums incorporated into our cocktail program at Jack Allen's. White Hat Rum out of Manor has a rich molasses quality that is perfect for our Manor Punch *(see page 88)*. And Treaty Oak Distillery recently released a barrel-aged rum that's good enough to drink straight up.

In the tequila category, it gets a little tricky. Since tequila can be made only in the Jalisco state of Mexico, along with a handful of adjoining counties, Texans have to get creative about how to produce and label it "tequila." But that certainly hasn't stopped us. Almost a dozen Texas producers have forged relationships with blue agave growers and production facilities in order to make authentic tequila marketed by Texans. Each fall, Jack Allen's hosts a patio party with Z Tequila, and we also make a number of cocktails with Dulce Vida and 512 Tequila.

Our policy for serving liquor from Texas distillers is very much the same as it has been for our farmers. If you've got something you want us to try, bring it in. Our doors are open. We'll try it and, if we think it's good, put it on the shelf. We'll give it a shot with our customers and see how it is received. So far, we've seen a lot of success.

If you've got something you want us to try, bring it in. Our doors are open.

BOTTOM RIGHT PHOTO BY LAURA MERIANS; TOP LEFT PHOTO BY BOB STICKNEY

Beet Tostadas

MAKES 12-16

We served this at an event for *Edible Austin* magazine one year. It is like a chicken chalupa but with beets. We roasted golden beets, chopped them up, and put them in this nice marinade. Then we blended goat cheese with a little olive oil, cream cheese, balsamic vinegar, and some crunchy basil seeds and made a smear. We put that on a cracker with the beets, some arugula, and a little chile oil, and people went crazy for it. It's the perfect appetizer for fall, and I guarantee you won't be able to stop with just one.

MARINADED BEETS

INGREDIENTS	MEASURE	CUT	PREPARATION
Golden beets	4 to 5		(1) In covered pot, cook whole beets in salted water until fork-tender, approximately 40 minutes, drain, and let rest 10 minutes. (2) Peel (should peel easily), slice into bite-size pieces, and place in glass bowl.
Fennel seeds Caraway seeds Mustard seeds Coriander seeds Cumin seeds Kosher salt	1 teaspoon 1 teaspoon 1 teaspoon 1 teaspoon 1 teaspoon 1 tablespoon		(3) In pan on stovetop, roast seeds until aromatic, 4 to 5 minutes. (4) Grind with salt to fine in coffee grinder, and add to beets.
Olive oil Sherry vinegar, good quality	1 cup 1/3 cup		(5) Add oil and vinegar to beets, mix well to marinade, and set aside.

BEETS I love beets. They have a beautiful texture and sweetness that is just so unique. We use all three varieties, the purple, the golden, and the chioggia, which most people call a "candy stripe" beet because of its pink and white stripes. They're all good for different reasons, but my favorite is the golden beet. It's the sweetest. And for some reason, because it's yellowish, people aren't as hesitant about it as they are purple beets, whose canned version has brought nightmares to children for generations. The golden beets are just beautiful.

HUMMUS

INGREDIENTS	MEASURE	CUT		PREPARATION
Garbanzo beans (chickpeas)	16-ounce can	Drained and rinsed		(1) For hummus, blend beans and next 6 ingredients in food processor until smooth.
Goat cheese	½ cup			
Lemon juice	3 to 5 tablespoons, to taste			
Tahini	1 ½ tablespoons			
Garlic cloves	3			
Roasted red bell pepper or pimiento, jarred	½ cup	Drained		
Kosher salt	½ teaspoon			
Olive oil	½ to 1 cup		*Add oil until you get the consistancy you want.*	(2) Slowly drizzle oil into hummus while blending on low for 1 to 2 minutes, until thoroughly mixed and smooth, and season to taste.
Salt and pepper	To taste			
Tostadas, your favorite				(3) To compose, spread hummus on tostadas, top with beets, drizzle with vinegar, and garnish with greens. And you can't go wrong with more goat cheese crumbles.
Balsamic vinegar	Drizzle			
Basil, arugula, or microgreens, fresh				
Goat cheese, crumbled	For garnish			

Fried Onion Rings

Artichoke Gratin

Beet Tostadas

Artichoke Gratin

SERVES 8-12

There's no getting around it: This dish is not healthy in any way. But it sure is good. We use sweet Gulf blue crab, local spinach (when it's in season), and artichokes from Two Happy Children Farms and bake it all in a Parmesan cream sauce. When it's piping hot, slather it on a toasted crostini, and it's heavenly. This is a great ice breaker to serve as an appetizer, and for me, it's a perfect way to feature Texas crab.

INGREDIENTS	MEASURE	CUT	PREPARATION
Butter Shallots	2 tablespoons 1 tablespoon	 Diced	(1) In pan, melt butter on medium heat, add shallots, and sweat for 2 to 3 minutes.
Garlic Flour	1 tablespoon 1 tablespoon	Chopped	(2) Stir in garlic and flour to make roux, for 2 to 3 minutes.
Half and half White wine Chipotle purée Artichoke juice (reserved from jar)	2 cups ¼ cup 1 teaspoon ½ cup		(3) Add half and half and next 3 ingredients, and reduce for 4 to 5 minutes, until thickened.
Spinach Kosher salt White pepper Cayenne pepper Nutmeg	3 cups 1 teaspoon 1 teaspoon 1 teaspoon 1 teaspoon	Chopped	(4) Reduce heat to low, add spinach and seasonings, and wilt spinach for approximately 4 minutes. (5) Set aside and allow to cool.
Parmesan cheese Artichoke hearts	2 cups 4 cups	Grated Drained, rinsed, and quartered	(6) Butter 13 x 9 casserole dish, and preheat oven to 400 degrees. (7) Mix Parmesan and artichoke hearts well, and place in dish along with spinach mixture.
Crabmeat	½ pound	Picked well for shells	(8) Top casserole with crabmeat.
Parmesan cheese Panko breadcrumbs	1 cup 1 cup	Grated	(9) Mix Parmesan with breadcrumbs, and sprinkle over casserole. (10) Bake for 30 minutes, until golden brown.

Fried Onion Rings

SERVES 2-4

Who doesn't love onion rings? Just make a bunch and dip 'em in ketchup. We make them specifically for our Steak Salad and one of our burgers, but really they're great on a lot of things. First, we start off with the perfect onion. Ten months out of the year we can get the Texas 1015 onion, and we slice them thin and separate out the rings. Then we soak them in 100 percent buttermilk—that's what crisps them. A little chile dust, with chile powder, flour, and other seasonings, gives them a kick. The key is to use a big pot so that it doesn't overflow or make a mess. You can use the same breading for chicken-fried anything.

INGREDIENTS	MEASURE	CUT	PREPARATION
Onion	1	Sliced very thin and separated into rings	(1) Place onions in bowl and pour in buttermilk to cover; allow to soak 5 minutes.
Buttermilk	Quantity to cover onions		
Vegetable oil	Enough to fill 2 inches in skillet		(2) In 6-inch-deep pot, heat oil to 350 degrees. (3) Remove single rings, allow to drain 1 minute, then mix in flour with dry hand. (4) In sifter shake to remove excess flour. (5) Fry 6 to 8 rings per batch until golden brown, using slotted spoon to keep them separate. (6) Drain on paper towel on plate.
Seasoned flour *(see recipe below)*	2 ½ cups		

SEASONED FLOUR (MAKES 2 ½ CUPS)

INGREDIENTS	MEASURE	CUT	PREPARATION
Flour	2 cups		(1) In bowl, using hands combine all ingredients well.
Black pepper	2 tablespoons	Ground	
Kosher salt	1 tablespoon		
Garlic salt	2 teaspoons		
Onion salt	2 teaspoons		
Cayenne	2 teaspoons		

TWO HAPPY CHILDREN FARM

When John and Yen Selking first met years ago, while working at a large corporation, the furthest thing from their minds was running a farm. John was an engineer and Yen was in research, but after they married and started a family, they felt the tug of a new direction in life. It began when the Selkings scouted for land north of Austin as an investment and settled on a 90-acre plot near Taylor.

At first, the Selkings used the land to escape from city life. John maintained his job while Yen stayed home with their two children, son Ryan and daughter Robyn. They got a few cows as a source for hormone-free meat and slowly began to sell their beef at the Georgetown farmers market. But eventually the cows became more of a burden than the Selkings anticipated and they switched their agricultural hobby to vegetables. All the while, the thing that stood out most to John and Yen was how happy they were on the farm. Even more fulfilling was seeing how happy the farm made their children, which is what led them to name the special place Two Happy Children Farm.

Within a few years, John's corporate career took a pause, giving him the chance to consider the potential this evolving farm could have for his family. Selking had grown up in the industry. His father owned a hog operation in Hebron, Illinois, and as the middle son of five children, John had certainly rolled up his sleeves and gotten his hands dirty.

"My mom kept a huge garden too. Farming was all around us," says Selking. "And when you are a farm kid, you end up with a bucket in your hand whether you like it or not."

Though he later chose engineering for a career, his affinity for Two Happy Children Farm quickly revealed that the life of farming was in his blood. Even when John and Yen fully committed to running the farm as a livelihood, they had a lot to learn.

"There's a big gap between when I grew up and when we started this farm," says John. "A lot has changed and I had to update my skills quickly."

But as Yen sees it, the leap into farming was well worth it.

"We own our farm and are our own boss," she says. "And we love what we're doing when we're in the field, even when it's 100 degrees or freezing outside. This is our living now, and it's better than being cooped up in an office all day long. It's a great feeling to be out in the fresh air all the time."

The primary goal is to model the 30 planted acres with seasonal crops based on what customers need most. During the winter, that means vegetables like cauliflower and broccoli. In spring, it's strawberries and artichokes. Summer brings tomatoes, watermelons, and sweet corn, while the fall consists of kale and spinach. And the Selking's children are a big part of making that happen.

Two Happy Children Farms sells most of its produce through four Central Texas farmers markets, including Barton Creek, Cedar Park, Georgetown, and Sun City. And a lot of it also goes to Jack Allen's Kitchen.

"I'll never forget the first time I saw Jack," says John. "Here's this guy, walking through the farmers market, who looked like Sammy Hagar from Van Halen with a bunch of bags in his hands filled with all sorts of produce. We were like, 'Where's he going with all that?' We thought he was so cool. And when we met him, we were struck by how friendly and happy he was. We've been friends ever since."

"I'll never forget the first time I saw Jack," says John. "Here's this guy, walking through the farmers market, who looked like Sammy Hagar from Van Halen . . ."

While Two Happy Children sources to a few other restaurants, Jack Allen's is one of its top priorities. Yen and John do their best to deliver their earliest, best crop as the seasons change so that the restaurant can quickly transition its seasonal menu.

And while the Selkings enjoy their relationship with Jack Allen's Kitchen as a long-term customer, they also reap the benefits of living minutes from the restaurant's Round Rock location. They explore seasonal specials, but they also love standbys: John orders stuffed pork, Yen likes chicken-fried chicken, Robyn's favorite is chicken-fried beef ribs, and Ryan goes for the Fat Jack burger.

Steak Salad

When we were first developing the Jack Allen's menu, we wanted a solution for those who like a good steak but are watching their carb intake. Also, I like serving a warm protein on a cold salad, for the contrast. We lay a nice tenderloin or New York strip on the salad. I love the crunchiness of the romaine and the spiciness of the arugula. We also use fresh radishes, watermelon radishes in the right season, which look beautiful on the salad. We originally served it with Gorgonzola cheese, but too many people asked to have that cut, so now we just suggest it to kick up the salad. Finished with a handful of crispy onion rings, it might just be the perfect salad.

STEAK SALAD MARINADE

INGREDIENTS	MEASURE	CUT	PREPARATION
Soy sauce	2 tablespoons		(1) For steak marinade, in stainless steel bowl combine first 6 ingredients using wire whisk.
Sea salt, smoked	½ teaspoon		
Olive oil	1 ¼ cup		
Worcestershire sauce	1 tablespoon		
Sambal chile sauce	1 tablespoon		
Garlic, fresh	1 tablespoon	Chopped	
Beef tenderloin	1 ½ pounds	Thinly sliced	(2) Add beef to mixture, and allow to marinate for a day but no more than 24 hours. (3) In cast-iron skillet on high heat, sear meat, separating with tongs, for 2 minutes on each side until cooked medium with good crispy edges. (4) Remove meat, allow to rest, and reserve for salad.

SALAD

INGREDIENTS	MEASURE	CUT	PREPARATION
Romaine lettuce	1 head	Chopped	(3) In large stainless steel bowl using tongs, thoroughly mix greens, radishes, and dressing from edges to middle. (4) Distribute salad among plates and place steak on top.
Arugula	¼ pound		
Radishes	5	Sliced	
Mustard Caper Dressing (opposite)	¾ cup		
Fried Onion Rings (see page 191)			(5) Top with onion rings.

Mustard Caper Dressing

MAKES 3½ CUPS

For the steak salad, we needed the right dressing to bring a good balance to the steak. Mustard is a perfect pairing, so we made a vinaigrette and punched it up with capers for a little extra acid. The dressing adds more zing to the salad, and together it all works really well.

INGREDIENTS	MEASURE	CUT	PREPARATION
Garlic	1 tablespoon	Chopped	(1) Combine first 7 ingredients slowly with immersion blender.
Dijon mustard	2 tablespoons		
Rice wine vinegar	½ cup		
Soy sauce	2 tablespoons		
Sesame oil	1 teaspoon		
Balsamic vinegar	¼ cup		
Honey	2 tablespoons		
Olive oil	2 cups		(2) Slowly add oil while using mixer until very smooth.
Capers, rinsed	½ cup		(3) With spoon, mix capers into dressing, cover, and refrigerate until use.

ARUGULA, a fall green, is always peppery, spicy, and clean. I like to use it as a canvas for spicy and sweet dressings, like the one in our Steak Salad as well as a smaller garnish salad for our Stuffed Texas Quail and Fried Green Tomatoes. But it also makes a nice pesto, and I always make sure I toss it into a batch of mixed greens because it adds a little extra depth.

We get a lot of our arugula from Animal Farms, which is a family farm in Cat Spring near Brenham. Animal Farms grows all sorts of organic produce but mainly specializes in lettuce and arugula. There's something extra flavorful about the arugula they grow. I love it.

Cornbread

Steak Salad with Mustard Caper Dressing

Spiced Carrot Soup
Turkey White Bean Chili

Spiced Carrot Soup

SERVES 4-6

Fresh carrots have a natural sweetness that's hard to beat, especially when you roast or caramelize them. I like spicy and sweet together, so we add a few spices to this to balance the sweetness. You could easily use butternut squash, pumpkin, or sweet potato if you're making this in the fall or winter. Serve it with some good crusty bread, and it's a satisfying meal.

INGREDIENTS	MEASURE	CUT		PREPARATION
Carrots	1 pound	Peeled and rough chopped	**Can substitute sweet potato, pumpkin, or butternut squash for carrots.*	(1) Preheat oven to 400 degrees. (2) On sheet pan, mix carrots, oil, and curry powder and roast for approximately 30 minutes.
Olive oil	2 teaspoons			
Curry powder	2 teaspoons			
Onion	1 cup	Chopped		(3) In large stockpot on medium heat, simmer carrots with remaining ingredients except garnishes until onion is tender, approximately 20 minutes. (4) Blend with immersion blender until smooth.
Chicken broth (boxed is fine)	4 cups			
Garlic	2 tablespoons	Chopped		
Kosher salt	1 teaspoon			
Pepper	1 teaspoon			
OPTIONAL GARNISHES: Chopped bacon, crispy prosciutto, Basil Oil *(see page 38)*, sour cream, or plain Greek yogurt				(5) Serve warm with optional garnish.

CARROTS When you're talking carrots, it's not just about the big old ruddy orange sticks that Bugs Bunny eats. Now we're talking all sorts of colors and sizes: orange, purple, white, and even rainbow, which makes it more fun visually for cooking. We do a lot of grilling, roasting, and pickling with carrots. And, of course, carrot cakes and breads.

When they first come out in the season, they're just sort of okay, but it's interesting to taste them as we move on into winter. They get sweeter and sweeter until we stop getting them in the spring.

I'm a big fan of baby carrots, which are picked earlier. They don't develop the bitterness that larger carrots can, and you don't have to peel them. They're ready to pop in your mouth right out of the ground—though you may want to rinse the dirt off first.

When farmers arrange their crops, they can time which rows will be picked as baby carrots and which ones they'll let grow longer.

For cooking, carrots are so versatile. They can act in the background as flavoring for a stock or soup, or they can take center stage in a roasted vegetable medley or as a spicy grilled side dish. Carrots have a little bit of everything: texture, a slightly sweet taste, beautiful color, and great versatility.

Turkey White Bean Chili

SERVES 6-8

I love chili. It's a great one-pot meal. Using turkey is my way, psychologically, of making chili healthy. But by no means is it really that healthy. I was just trying to use a protein other than red meat or pork. But with everything else in it, it's still a little bad for you. And I'm okay with that. We spice it up with green chiles and use white beans for creaminess. Super healthy? Maybe not. Delicious? Definitely.

INGREDIENTS	MEASURE	CUT	PREPARATION
White beans, dry	4 cups		(1) In soup pot on medium heat, cook beans in water until tender, 50 to 60 minutes, and drain.
Water	3 quarts		
Bacon	6 strips	Diced	(2) In another soup pot on medium heat, sauté bacon and onion until slightly browned.
Onion	3 cups	Diced	
Turkey	1 pound	Ground	(3) Add turkey to bacon pot, and cook for 20 to 30 minutes, stirring to separate turkey.
Garlic	¼ cup	Peeled and chopped	(4) Add beans and remaining ingredients to bacon pot, and cook for 20 to 30 minutes. (5) Season to taste. Tortillas will thicken soup; add more water or broth if necessary.
Tortilla, corn	4	Chopped	
Bay leaves	2		
Tomatillo Sauce *(see page 224)*	4 cups		
Oregano	1 tablespoon	Ground	
Cumin	1 tablespoon	Ground	
Coriander	1 tablespoon	Ground	
Chicken broth (boxed is fine)	4 cups		
Salt and pepper	To taste		

Tamale Jalapeño-Cornbread Dressing

SERVES 8-12

This is a recipe that Kitty Crider, the former food critic for the *Austin American-Statesman,* picked as one of her Top 10 Recipes of All Time. It's really a celebration of corn. It starts with a good homemade cornbread that's full of flavor and sweet. Then we add crumbled corn chips for crunch. And the tamale weaves in that rich flavor of masa. It's corn from a few different directions that brings real versatility of flavor. Putting that all together at the Thanksgiving table is just a good idea.

INGREDIENTS	MEASURE	CUT		PREPARATION
Butter	6 tablespoons			(1) In large heavy skillet over medium heat, melt butter, add vegetables and herbs, and sauté until tender, approximately 15 minutes.
Onions	1 ½ cups	Chopped		
Red bell peppers	1 ½ cups	Chopped		
Poblano peppers	2 cups	Chopped		
Jalapeños	3 large	Stemmed, seeded, and chopped		
Sage, fresh (can substitute with dried sage)	1 tablespoon	Chopped		
Oregano, dried	1 ½ tablespoons			
Cornbread *(opposite)*	1 pound	Broken up		(2) Place cornbread in large bowl, and stir in pepper mixture.
Cilantro, fresh	¼ cup	Chopped		(3) Mix in cilantro and next 4 ingredients. (4) Preheat oven to 325 degrees, and butter a 13 x 9 baking dish.
Corn chips	1 ½ cups	Crushed		
Corn kernels, fresh or frozen (thaw before baking)	1 ½ cups			
Cream-style canned corn	1 ½ cups			
Chicken broth (boxed is fine)	3 cups	Heated		
Tamales	1 dozen	Shuck removed and chopped into 1-inch pieces	**If stuffing seems dry, add more butter.*	(4) Stir tamale pieces into dressing, season to taste, place in baking dish with foil cover, and bake approximately 45 minutes. (5) Remove foil, and bake 15 minutes, until stuffing has browned.
Salt and pepper	To taste			

Cornbread

If you have a handful of standard recipes for your collection, a good cornbread needs to be one of them. And if you make a big batch of cornbread at home, you better have something to do with it once it gets cold. That's why we came up with the Tamale Jalapeño-Cornbread Dressing *(opposite)* and the Sweet Corn Tamale *(see page 236).* It lets you use the leftovers in a much more creative and flavorful way. You can also just cut the cornbread up into smaller cubes and toast them for a salad.

INGREDIENTS	MEASURE	CUT	PREPARATION
Cornmeal	1 ½ cup		(1) Butter 13 x 9 pan, and preheat oven to 400 degrees, 375 degrees for convection oven. (2) In small bowl, combine first 6 ingredients.
Flour	1 ½ cup		
Sugar	⅓ cup plus 1 tablespoon		
Baking powder	1 tablespoon		
Baking soda	1 tablespoon		
Salt	¼ teaspoon		
Yogurt, plain	1 cup	*Test for doneness by sticking toothpick in center; it should come out clean.*	(3) In large bowl, whisk remaining ingredients together. (4) Stir in dry ingredients to form batter, and pour into pan. (5) Bake for 16 minutes, turning pan halfway through for even cooking.
Cream corn	⅓ cup plus 1 tablespoon		
Corn, frozen	⅓ cup plus 1 tablespoon		
Buttermilk	1 ½ cup		
Eggs	3		
Butter, melted	⅓ cup plus 1 tablespoon

Clockwise from above: Pumpkin Goat Cheese Tart (page 245); Tamale Jalapeño-Cornbread Dressing; Cornbread; Sweet Potato Bourbon Gratin; Turkey and Dressing Meatballs with Maple Giblet Gravy; Texas Pecan Cranberry Chutney.

Sweet Potato Bourbon Gratin

SERVES 6-8

This is simply a play on the regular potato gratin but—with the holiday season and the availability of sweet potatoes at that time of year—we suggest this as an alternative to canned yams in a casserole dish with marshmallows on top. Add bourbon and pecans to the mix, and Thanksgiving just got fancy. It's great for serving at a big meal because it needs 20 to 30 minutes out of the oven to set up, which gives you time to finish other items you may be cooking.

INGREDIENTS	MEASURE	CUT	PREPARATION
Heavy cream Bourbon Cinnamon, ground Allspice Nutmeg Kosher salt Pepper	2 cups 1/4 cup 1 1/4 teaspoon 1/4 teaspoon 1/4 teaspoon 1 teaspoon 1 teaspoon		(1) In large mixing bowl, whisk together cream and next 6 ingredients thoroughly.
Sweet potatoes	4 medium	Peeled and thinly sliced to 1/8 inch	(2) Preheat oven to 375 degrees, and butter a 10-inch-square baking dish. (3) Place layer of sweet potatoes in dish, and drizzle 1/4 cup of cream mixture over it. (4) Repeat 2 times, pressing down each time.
Pecans	1 cup	Chopped	(4) Top with pecans, cover with foil, and bake for 30 minutes. (5) Remove foil and bake until cream is absorbed and surface is golden brown, 15 to 20 minutes. Let rest 15 to 30 minutes before slicing.

SWEET POTATOES Texas can grow some amazing sweet potatoes. From Comanche down to Poteet and even in parts of Stonewall and Fredericksburg, you'll find farmers pulling these guys out of the ground in the fall. I usually skip the really big ones and go for the smaller ones, 12 to 16 ounces. They're sweeter and have the best flavor.

The lazy way to treat them is just to throw them in the oven and bake them for about half an hour. Or you could boil and mash. The problem is, most people think that you have to make it sweeter. They add too much brown sugar or maple syrup, and that's just not the way to go. I like sweet potato desserts, but to really get the genuine beauty out of the sweet potato, let it stand on its own. There's nothing better than a plain baked sweet potato with a little butter and a sprinkle of salt.

We treat the sweet potato similar to squash. We roast it and put it in a hash or make it a smear to add a sweet component to a savory dish. And don't neglect the greens of the sweet potato. It can be cost prohibitive for farmers to save and wash the greens for you to use, so they often just compost them. But if you can get greens, braise them like you would any other green and you'll discover a sweetness to them that's really nice.

Texas Pecan Cranberry Chutney

SERVES 6-8

Cranberries are a natural fall ingredient. But they don't grow in Texas, so I like to put them with a few ingredients that are native to the state: pecans and citrus. I soften the cranberries with fresh orange juice, which counteracts the bitterness of the berry. I also add a little local honey, but you really don't need much. After you cook it with all the ingredients, it needs a little texture and crunch, so I fold in Texas pecans. This beats canned cranberry sauce any day of the week.

INGREDIENTS	MEASURE	CUT	PREPARATION
Water	1 cup		(1) In medium saucepan over medium heat, bring water and sugar to boil.
Sugar	¾ cup		
Cranberries, fresh	12 ounces		(2) Add cranberries and next 7 ingredients, bring to boil, then simmer for 10 minutes.
Apples	1 cup	Peeled, cored, and diced	
Cider vinegar	½ cup		
Orange juice	1 cup		
Raisins	½ cup		
Cinnamon	½ teaspoon		
Ginger	½ teaspoon	Ground	
Allspice	¼ teaspoon	Ground	
Pecans, roasted	1 cup		(3) Remove from heat, cool slightly, and add pecans and zest. Can be served at room temperature or cold.
Orange zest	2 tablespoons		

TEXAS PECANS I don't want to put my foot in it with Georgia or Alabama, or even Louisiana, but to me there is nothing better than a good Texas pecan. Texas is a better region for growing. Pecan farmers are everywhere in Central Texas. San Saba is the self-proclaimed Pecan Capital of the World. But when there's a bad year, those suckers can get expensive. The best way to get around that is just to buy the pieces. You don't need the halves unless you want to make something beautiful.

We buy nothing but Texas pecans because they can easily be stored throughout the year. They're a natural protein to add heft to a dish, and their texture is great for adding crunch and nuttiness. While there's nothing like sitting on the porch and shelling a few pecans to enjoy with a nice glass of bourbon, we use them at the restaurant to crust chicken and fish, for chutneys and relishes, and, of course, for desserts.

Turkey and Dressing Meatballs with Maple Giblet Gravy

SERVES 4-6

This was a last-minute idea we did for an event one time. We took all the best things about Thanksgiving and made it into an appetizer. It's a great way to use leftovers, that's for sure. Just put turkey and stuffing together, roll it in a ball, and bake it. Serve it with Maple Giblet Gravy, and you'll have something to be thankful for all over again.

MEATBALLS

INGREDIENTS	MEASURE	CUT	PREPARATION
Celery Onion Dijon mustard Turkey leftovers Tamale and Jalapeño-Cornbread Dressing, leftover *(see page 202)* Worcestershire sauce Eggs, beaten	¼ cup ½ cup 1 tablespoons 1 pound 2 cups 1 tablespoon 3	Diced Diced Diced	(1) Preheat oven to 375 degrees, and butter a sheet pan. (2) In large mixing bowl using hands, combine all ingredients and mix well. (3) Form mixture into 1-inch balls, place on pan, and bake for 20 to 25 minutes, until lightly browned.

MAPLE GIBLET GRAVY

INGREDIENTS	MEASURE	CUT	PREPARATION
Butter Onions	2 tablespoons ¼ cup	 Diced	(1) In saucepan, sauté butter and onions.
Flour	2 tablespoons		(2) Gradually whisk flour into onions for approximately 2 minutes.
Chicken broth (boxed is fine) Giblets, cooked	3 cups ½ cup	 Chopped	(3) Add broth and giblets to onion mixture, and cook on medium heat until slightly thickened, approximately 10 minutes.
Maple syrup Sage, fresh Salt and pepper	¼ cup 1 tablespoon To taste	 Chopped	(4) Add syrup and sage to saucepan, and season to taste.

W

Oyster Dressing

Grilled Spiced Carrots

Roasted Root Vegetables

Grilled Spiced Carrots

SERVES 4

If you grow carrots in your garden or have a bunch of them from the farmers market, it's good to have a few ways to prepare them. This is one of my favorites, another way I like to play with sweet and spicy components. Carrots lend themselves to a spicy rub. The added bonus with this is the grill. It gives you a nice smokiness that adds a lot of depth to the carrots. This is a go-to side for almost any grilled meat, like steak or pork chops.

INGREDIENTS	MEASURE	CUT	PREPARATION
Fennel seeds, whole Coriander, whole Cumin seeds, whole Mustard seeds, whole Red chile flakes Black peppercorns Allspice	½ teaspoon ½ teaspoon ½ teaspoon ½ teaspoon ½ teaspoon ½ teaspoon ½ teaspoon		(1) In 10-inch skillet, roast first 7 spices until fragrant.
Paprika Turmeric	3 teaspoons 1 teaspoon		(2) Grind spices in coffee grinder; combine with paprika and turmeric.
Baby carrots Olive oil Kosher salt	1 pound 2 tablespoons Pinch, to taste	Washed	(3) Prepare grill to high heat. (4) Toss carrots in olive oil, spices, and salt to coat well. (5) Place on grill and turn every couple of minutes until cooked through, approximately 10 minutes.

Oyster Dressing

SERVES 8-12

This may be my son Bryce's favorite thing on Thanksgiving. It's inspired by a New Orleans–style Southern recipe. Oysters are easy to get around the holidays, and if you love them, get them. When we're serving a big meal for a lot of people, I like having a few dressings for people to try. The biggest hassle for holiday cooking is that you're competing for time in the oven. But this works when you serve it 30 to 45 minutes after you've taken it out of the oven. And the day after, throw this in a skillet or microwave and serve it with gravy—it's next-day delicious.

INGREDIENTS	MEASURE	CUT	PREPARATION
Bacon, slab	4 slices	Diced into ¼-inch pieces	(1) In saucepan on medium heat, slightly brown bacon, stirring approximately 1 minute.
Butter	½ cup		(2) Add butter and vegetables to bacon, and lightly brown, for 5 minutes. (3) Preheat oven to 350 degrees and butter a 10 x 14 baking dish.
Celery	¼ cup	Diced into ¼-inch pieces	
Green bell pepper	½ cup	Diced into ¼-inch pieces	
Onion	½ cup	Finely diced	
Garlic	2 tablespoons	Chopped	
Cornbread *(see page 203)*	½ pound	Broken up	(4) In large bowl, combine breads and oysters, and set aside.
French bread, dried	½ pound	Diced into ¼-inch pieces	
Oysters, shucked	4 dozen, plus 2 cups reserved liquid		
Eggs, slightly beaten	4		(5) In bowl, mix together remaining ingredients, then combine with cornbread mixture. (6) Pour into baking dish and bake for 45 minutes, until crisp on top. Let rest for 30 minutes before serving.
Paprika	2 tablespoons		
Garlic powder	1 teaspoon		
Cayenne pepper	1 teaspoon		
Green onions	¼ cup	Chopped	
Parsley	2 tablespoons	Chopped	
Tabasco	1 teaspoon		
Kosher salt	1 teaspoon		

Roasted Root Vegetables

SERVES 8-12

Root vegetables all play well together in the same dish. And roasting them is the best way to bring out a whole range of natural flavors. From a home-cook standpoint, if you don't like turnips, leave them out, but keep everything else to get the most out of this quick and easy casserole. Make sure you cut the vegetables into similar sizes so that they cook evenly.

INGREDIENTS	MEASURE	CUT
Carrots, baby	8 to 12	Trimmed
Turnips, baby	8 to 12	Peeled and cut in half
Sweet potatoes	2 medium	Peeled and cut into bite-size pieces
Butternut squash	1 medium	Peeled, seeded, and chopped in small wedges
Potatoes	8 to 11 small	Cleaned and cut in half
Parsnips	2	Peeled, trimmed, and cut in half
Red onions	2 medium	Quartered
Garlic cloves	8	
Rosemary, fresh	1 sprig	
Thyme, fresh	1 sprig	
Sage, fresh	1 sprig	
Salt and pepper to taste		
Olive oil	½ cup	

PREPARATION

(1) Preheat oven to 400 degrees. (2) In large mixing bowl, thoroughly combine all ingredients to coat well. (3) Place on sheet pan in oven, and stir occasionally while roasting until golden and tender, approximately 45 minutes.

WINTER SQUASH AND PUMPKIN

The fall is when we see the heartier squash, as opposed to summer's yellow crookneck and zucchini. It's butternut, acorn, and spaghetti squash. But you can't forget pumpkin. It's a squash too. We treat it just like a butternut squash and often roast it and cut it up for a hash, a smear, or a soup. Because people associate pumpkin with sweetness, I often just describe it as "winter squash" when writing it up for a menu item.

The key to cooking with pumpkin is getting the right size. It has to be small or medium, not the size you use to carve a Jack-o'-lantern. They don't have as much flavor when they are big. Plus, they're a pain to clean. If you've never tried it before, just seed and halve a small one, and roast it face-up on a pan. You'll see pumpkin in a whole new way.

FARMER
PARKING
ONLY
ALL OTHERS
WILL BE
PLANTED

OAK HILL FARMS SPINACH

For most Texans, the small town of Poteet, just 30 miles south of San Antonio, means one thing during spring: strawberries. Historically, the rural town has garnered a reputation for its seasonal bounty of the luscious fruit, with an annual festival to celebrate its harvest. But Jack Gilmore is more interested in an altogether different crop: spinach. It begins its harvest at Poteet's Oak Hill Farms late in the fall.

The lush leafy green is a hot commodity for Jack Allen's Kitchen each fall, as the restaurant rotates in its signature Navajo Tacos. Carried over from Jack's days at Z Tejas, the Navajo Taco is a Southwestern tostada stacked with rice, beans, roasted chicken, pico de gallo, and green mole sauce. But the defining ingredient is the crunchy flash-fried Parmesan-dusted spinach that garnishes the dish. And for the Navajo Taco, not just any spinach will do.

"The only spinach we can deep fry is really thick, crinkly, and perfect," says Jack. "It has a certain texture, and the only place I can find it is at Cora and Bob Lamar's Oak Hill Farms."

Cora and Bob have farmed throughout Texas for about 45 years. They started in cattle and transitioned to produce when the ranching industry took a bad turn. They have farmed near Waco and Austin but settled a couple of decades ago in Poteet to create Oak Hill Farms, where they cultivate more than 50 varieties of vegetables and fruits on more than 200 acres.

"When people ask us what we do for farming, my answer is always 'What don't we do?'" says Cora. "Of course, we do strawberries in the spring because this is Poteet, but we do just about everything else as well."

Both Cora and Bob come from farming families, so working the land is in their blood.

"I don't think you ever stop learning about farming," says Cora. "It's not something you can just pick up by reading about it in a book. You learn by trial and error and by putting a crop in by the skin of your teeth. The key is to turn your crops, and you've got to let the earth have a chance to build back up."

In their many years as a farming operation, the Lamars have come to understand how to sell. "Anybody can grow something," says Cora. "But you better know how to market. You better have it sold before you put it in the ground, or you're wasting your time."

Considering her largest customer for the past 25 years has been HEB, one of the state's largest grocery-store chains, Lamar's business savvy rings true. A few years ago, she struck up a relationship with John Lash of Farm to Table *(see page 95)*, a delivery business that sells produce from Central Texas farms to area restaurants. The connection opened new doors for Oak Hill Farms, including a regular account with Jack Allen's Kitchen and, particularly, for that thick, crinkly fall spinach.

"It's more than just the spinach itself that's so great," says Jack. "It's how Cora takes care of it. It's triple-washed, dried, and ready to use by the time it gets to me. She knows exactly what she's doing, and that's what makes me a loyal customer. Cora's got me hooked on the good stuff, what can I say?"

Cora and Bob see Oak Hill Farms as something more than just a livelihood. Their children and grandchildren also work the farm, so it's a family endeavor, an investment not only in the seeds they put in the ground but in the loved ones around them.

"This is just our way of life, and I don't know anything else I'd rather be doing," says Cora. "Three things are important to me: my faith, my family, and my farm, in that order. It's really as simple as that."

"I don't think you ever stop learning about farming," says Cora. "It's not something you can just pick up by reading about it in a book."

Navajo Tacos

SERVES 4

The Navajo Taco is something that's part of who we are. Even though it started at Z Tejas, people would have revolted if we didn't bring it to Jack Allen's. At first it was just on a tortilla shell, but I started making a cross between pasta and bread that we fried. It was back when Southwest cuisine was the big thing, so I called it Navajo Bread. We stacked it with mole, beans, rice, corn, smoked chicken, and pico de gallo. But the key ingredient was the fried spinach, which was an accident, really. I was just playing around in the kitchen and wanted to find something to make crispy. I saw this mound of spinach, so I threw it in the fryer. It started bubbling and spitting everywhere and made a huge mess. But when I pulled it out 20 seconds later, it looked pretty cool and stayed really crispy. I added Parmesan and cornmeal for texture, and it became the garnish for the Navajo Taco. Everyone went crazy about it. It's my best accident ever! We serve it only in the fall, when we can get spinach from Cora Lamar of Oak Hill Farms. She has the perfect crinkle-cut spinach for frying. When it's in season, we probably go through 300 to 400 pounds a week, but that's not enough to keep up with the demand. We serve it only at lunch, and it's not uncommon for us to tell customers that we're out by 1:30. People get huffy about it, but they get it. It's a special dish, and they end up coming back for more.

INGREDIENTS	MEASURE	CUT	PREPARATION
Mole Verde Sauce *(see page 225)* Tomatillo Sauce *(see page 224)* Onions Bell peppers Chicken, roasted (your favorite)	3 cup 1 cup ¼ cup ¼ cup 2 cups	 Julienned Julienned Picked from bone	(1) In saucepan, combine first 5 ingredients and heat approximately 10 minutes.
Red cabbage Sour cream Navajo Bread *(opposite)* Crispy Fried Spinach *(see page 224)* Veggie Studded Rice *(see page 227)* Black Beans *(see page 226)*	1 cup ½ cup	Shredded	(2) Follow assembly directions on page 221, which includes quantities.

Navajo Bread

SERVES 4

INGREDIENTS	MEASURE	CUT	PREPARATION
Flour	2 cups		(1) In standup mixer on slow speed, combine first 6 ingredients for 1 minute, scraping sides with spatula as necessary.
Salt	1 teaspoon		
Sugar	1 teaspoon		
Cilantro	2 tablespoons	Finely chopped	
Basil, fresh	1 tablespoon	Finely chopped	
Rosemary, fresh	1 tablespoon	Finely chopped	
Water	1 cup		(2) While mixing, slowly add water to mixture until all is absorbed, approximately 1 minute. (3) Turn mixer to medium, and mix for 4 minutes so dough forms ball; add splashes of water if too dry. Let rest at least 1 hour before using.

TO FORM NAVAJO BREAD:

(1) Roll dough into 1-inch balls and dust with flour.
(2) Using pasta roller on #2 setting, run ball through to slightly flatten.
(3) Repeat on #3 setting, #4 setting, and #5 setting until round and thin like tortilla.

TO FRY:

(1) In 6-inch-deep pot, heat 2 inches vegetable oil to 350 degrees.
(2) Fry 1 tortilla at a time carefully until crispy, using tongs to flip, approximately 2 minutes each side.
(3) Remove and drain on paper towel.

TO ASSEMBLE TACOS:

(1) Place fry bread shell on plate, and top with ¼ of Crispy Fried Spinach.
(2) Top spinach with ¼ of chicken mixture.
(3) Randomly throw ¼ cup red cabbage on taco and add dollop of sour cream in center.
(4) On plate, mound Veggie Studded Rice *(see page 227)* on one end and Black Beans *(see page 226)* on the other and place the taco in between.

Navajo Bread
Mole Verde

Veggie Studded Rice and Black Beans
Crispy Fried Spinach

Crispy Fried Spinach

INGREDIENTS	MEASURE	CUT	PREPARATION
Parmesan	1 cup	Grated	(1) For Spinach Dust, mix together first 3 ingredients and set aside.
Cornmeal	1 cup	Fine ground	
White pepper	2 teaspoon		
Spinach, thick crinkle, with zero moisture	1 pound		(2) Follow frying directions below.
Vegetable oil	2 inches deep for your pot		

FOR FRYING:

Do only outside or in garage, with no children or pets around.
(1) In 12-inch-deep pot, heat vegetable oil to 350 degrees.
 WARNING: Spinach will make oil pop.
(2) Fry 4 ounces at a time carefully, using skimmer to move spinach around, for 20 to 30 seconds until crispy.
(3) Remove with skimmer to drain on paper towel.
(4) Place spinach in mixing bowl and toss gently with ¼ of Spinach Dust.
(5) Repeat 3 times.

Tomatillo Sauce

INGREDIENTS	MEASURE	CUT	PREPARATION
Tomatillos, peeled	2 pounds		(1) In stockpot, add water to barely cover first 5 ingredients, bring to boil, and cook for 2 minutes.
White onion	1 cup	Chopped	
Garlic	2 tablespoons	Chopped	
Salt	1 teaspoon		
White pepper	1 teaspoon		
Cilantro	1 cup	Chopped	(2) Remove from heat, and add cilantro. (3) Purée with immersion blender until smooth.

Cilantro Pesto

MAKES 4½ CUPS

INGREDIENTS	MEASURE	CUT	PREPARATION
Pumpkin seeds Sesame seeds	1 cup ½ cup		(1) Preheat oven to 300 degrees. (2) Place seeds on sheet pan and roast, approximately 10 minutes.
Vegetable oil White pepper Kosher salt Garlic, fresh	2 cups 1 teaspoon 1 teaspoon 4 cloves		(3) In food processor or blender, combine seeds, oil, and next 3 ingredients well until pumpkin seeds are chopped up.
Cilantro	¼ pound		(4) Slowly feed in cilantro, and purée until smooth.

Mole Verde Sauce

MAKES 3½ CUPS

INGREDIENTS	MEASURE	CUT	PREPARATION
Cilantro Pesto *(see above)*	1 cup		(1) In large bowl, combine all ingredients and blend with immersion blender until smooth.
Tomatillo Sauce *(see page 224)*	2 cups		
Honey	3 tablespoons		
Jalapeños	2 tablespoons	Washed, stemmed, and chopped	
Cumin	1 teaspoon		
Chile powder	½ teaspoon		

Black Beans

SERVES 8-12

The trick to cooking any type of bean is, simply, water. No salt or anything else. Just cover the beans with water, simmer, and two hours later, they're perfect. Okay, back up. When the beans are almost done, which means about 10 percent of the water is left, then add seasonings, fresh onions, and cilantro. Jack Allen's beans are completely vegetarian. You could use chicken broth at the end or add bacon or sausage, but we keep it simple.

INGREDIENTS	MEASURE	CUT	PREPARATION
Black beans Water	2 pounds 2 to 3 quarts		(1) In stockpot on medium heat, bring beans and water to boil. (2) Reduce heat and stir every 5 minutes with long spoon; add water as needed.
Yellow onions	2 cups	¼-inch diced	(3) When beans are half done (approximately 1 hour), add onions; continue stirring.
Garlic, fresh Kosher salt White pepper Oregano Cumin Cilantro	2 tablespoons 1 tablespoon 2 teaspoons 1 tablespoon 1 tablespoon 1 cup, packed	Chopped Ground Chopped	(4) When beans are slightly tender, add remaining ingredients and stir well. Cook 10 more minutes or until tender.

Veggie Studded Rice

SERVES 8-12

When we first started the restaurant, we wanted to vary the rice with seasonal vegetables but decided to stick with what's available most often, corn. We make white rice first. Then we add roasted corn—we roast corn every day for a lot of recipes—along with butter, cilantro, and green onions. Keep the rice and corn separate until after cooking, though, or the corn will turn to mush. You want that bright texture of corn and other ingredients, so mix it all together at the end.

INGREDIENTS	MEASURE	CUT	PREPARATION
Water White rice	4 cups 2 cups		(1) In medium saucepan, bring water to boil, add rice, stir with fork, and cover. (2) Reduce heat to low, and simmer for approximately 20 minutes, until liquid is absorbed; set aside.
Corn	2 ears, husks intact		(3) On prepared grill, cook corn in husks approximately 20 minutes, turning to cook evenly. (4) Using knife, shave kernels off cobs.
Cilantro Green onions Butter	½ cup ½ cup ¼ cup	Chopped Chopped Melted	(5) In large bowl, combine corn with cilantro, onions, and butter, then stir in rice.
Salt and pepper	To taste		(6) Season to taste.

Shrimp in Mojo de Ajo

SERVES 4

"Ajo" is Spanish for garlic. For this spicy dish, I wanted the garlic to shine through with the sweetness of the shrimp. This is more of a Southwestern version of scampi, but instead of butter and Parmesan, you're using the garlic and big robust spices. Serve this on our Veggie Studded Rice with some black beans on the side, and you've got a great meal.

INGREDIENTS	MEASURE	CUT	PREPARATION
Onion	1 medium	Chopped	**For Salsa Mojo de Ajo:** (1) In blender purée first 12 ingredients, and set aside.
Tomato, Roma	8	Chopped	
Chipotles, dried	4		
Garlic	4 cloves	Peeled and chopped	
Bay leaf	1		
Coriander leaves	1 tablespoon		
Oregano	1 tablespoon		
Cumin	1 tablespoon		
Kosher salt	1 ½ tablespoons		
White vinegar	¼ cup		
Olive oil	1 ½ cups		
Water	2 cups		
Butter	2 tablespoons		**For Shrimp:** (1) In heavy-duty saucepan on medium high heat, melt butter and add shrimp. (2) Cook until pink, approximately 2 minutes, then turn over. (3) Add 2 cups Salsa Mojo de Ajo to pan, cook approximately 2 minutes, and serve over Veggie Studded Rice or Cheesy Grits.
Shrimp	16 to 20 medium	Peeled and veined, with tail on	

Crispy Fried Oysters

SERVES 4

I love oysters. And there's nothing wrong with frying them up and popping them in your mouth. I have a tendency to fry these in a batter of cornmeal, which by itself can be coarse and gritty, so we cut it with flour. These are really simple to make if you're okay with frying in your house. And they're quick, perfect in 2 minutes. You can use any sort of dipping sauce, from cocktail sauce and ketchup to Sweet and Spicy Avocado Sauce *(see page 54),* but they also go really well on a salad or as a surf 'n turf addition to a grilled steak.

INGREDIENTS	MEASURE	CUT		PREPARATION
Yellow cornmeal, fine	1 cup			(1) In bowl, combine first 4 ingredients well, and set aside.
Flour, all purpose	2 cups			
Black pepper	1 tablespoon	Ground		
Kosher salt	1 tablespoon			
Oysters	2 dozen	Shelled and drained		(2) In another bowl, cover oysters with buttermilk, and allow to sit for 15 minutes.
Buttermilk	1 cup			
Vegetable oil	2 inches deep in pot		**Try this with Jalapeño Tartar Sauce (see page 270) too.*	(3) In 6-inch-deep pot, heat oil to 350 degrees. (4) Drain oysters, and place in breading, using both hands to totally coat. (5) Fry 6 to 8 oysters at a time, carefully, using slotted spoon to be sure they don't stick together, until crispy; drain on paper towels.

Stuffed Texas Quail

SERVES 6

Quail is easy to find in Texas, and this is a great way to use leftover dressing. The corn and tamales work well with this type of meat. Ask your butcher for a boneless bird, and that will be a lot easier to stuff and eat. One bird per person is plenty. It doesn't take that long to grill quail, so be careful not to overcook and dry it out. The stuffing should help keep it real moist.

INGREDIENTS	MEASURE	CUT	PREPARATION
Dried oregano, preferably Mexican	1½ tablespoons		**For Achiote Marinade:** (1) Using coffee grinder, grind together first 5 ingredients, then transfer to bowl and smash in achiote paste.
Black pepper	1½ tablespoons		
Cumin seeds	1¼ teaspoons		
Cloves, whole	½ teaspoon		
Cinnamon, preferably Mexican canela	1½ teaspoons		
Achiote paste	3 tablespoons		
Salt	1 tablespoon		(2) In blender, combine achiote mixture with salt, garlic, and juice, blend until smooth, with almost no grittiness, and reserve. See "Slow-Grilling the Quail," below.
Garlic cloves	14 large	Peeled and roughly chopped	
Fresh orange juice	1½ cups		
Tamale and Jalapeño-Cornbread Dressing *(see page 202)*	2 cups		(3) In large bowl, mix dressing and next 4 ingredients together until incorporated.
Celery	¼ cup	Diced	
Onions	¼ cup	Diced	
Jalapeño	2 tablespoons	Diced	
Egg, beaten	1		
Quail, semi-boneless	6 to 8		(4) Using hands, stuff quail, place on pan, and refrigerate for up to 1 hour.

SLOW-GRILLING THE QUAIL:

(1) Heat gas grill to medium-high, or light charcoal fire and begin when coals are covered with gray ash and very hot.
(2) Either turn center burner(s) to medium-low or bank coals for indirect cooking.
(3) Place quail on hot part of grill for 2 minutes, then turn over for 2 more minutes with lid closed.
(4) Move quail to coolest part of grill.
(5) Baste top of quail with Achiote Marinade.
(6) Close lid for approximately 5 minutes.
(7) Flip quail and generously baste with marinade again.
(8) Grill until quail is thoroughly tender: Work in a fork near the bone; the meat should easily come free.

Texas Quail Pibil

SERVES 4-6

We came up with this dish for a special tequila dinner promoting Lucinda Hutson's new book *Viva Tequila!: Cocktails, Cooking, and Other Agave Adventures.* Usually we do pibil with pork, but we decided to use quail because we have a great relationship with local purveyor Diamond H Ranch for Bandera quail. Plus, we thought it would match up well with a beer and tequila cocktail from Lucinda's book. This was also an opportunity to showcase summer corn, and the sweet corn tamale came out perfectly. It adds a dimension to the dish that sets it off really well.

INGREDIENTS	MEASURE	CUT	PREPARATION
Dried oregano, preferably Mexican Black pepper Cumin seeds Cloves, whole Cinnamon, preferably Mexican canela Achiote paste	1 1/2 tablespoons 1 1/2 tablespoons 1 1/4 teaspoons 1/2 teaspoon 1 1/2 teaspoons 3 tablespoons		**For Achiote Marinade:** (1) Using coffee grinder, grind together first 5 ingredients, then transfer to bowl and smash in achiote paste.
Salt Garlic cloves Fresh orange juice	1 tablespoon 14 large 1 1/2 cups	 Peeled and roughly chopped	(2) In blender, combine achiote mixture with salt, garlic, and juice, blend until smooth, with almost no grittiness, and reserve.
Quail, semi-boneless	8	Sliced 1/8 inch thick	**For the Quail:** (4) In large bowl or plastic food bag, combine quail and marinade, coating meat completely. Allow to marinate for several hours or overnight. See "Slow-Grilling the Quail" on page 233.
Red onions	2 large, or 1 pound		**For the Pickled Red Onions:** (5) Before you grill quail, prepare pickled red onions by pouring boiling water over them in non-aluminum bowl. (6) Wait 10 seconds, then strain.
Red wine vinegar Fresh orange juice Kosher salt	1/2 cup 2 cups 1 1/2 tsp		(7) Return onions to bowl, add vinegar and juice, and stir in salt. (8) Cover bowl, and set aside until serving as garnish for quail.

Sweet Corn Tamales

MAKES 1 TO 1½ DOZEN

The flavor of this tamale is rich and sweet. It goes well with anything a little bit spicy, like the Texas Quail Pibil. But you could also serve it with the Mojo de Ajo Shrimp or the Stuffed Texas Quail.

INGREDIENTS	MEASURE	CUT	PREPARATION
Corn, sweet	Approximately 5 ears; 6 cups kernels	Husks removed and placed in pot with water to cover; kernels cut from cob, lightly ground to medium coarse in food processor	(1) In large bowl, using hands mix ground corn kernels, masa, and water.
Corn masa	1 ½ cups		
Water, warm	1 cup		
Butter, room temperature	1 ¼ cup		(2) In another bowl with mixer or by hand, beat together butter and next 3 ingredients. (3) Stir mixture into corn mixture bowl.
Goat cheese	1 cup		
Sugar	½ cup		
Kosher salt	1 teaspoon		
Baking soda	1 teaspoon		(4) Add baking soda, and combine until mixture becomes thick batter.

PREPARING THE TAMALES:

(1) Remove softened husks from water and drain.
(2) Select husks to wrap tamales; use small husks to cover bottom of steamer.
(3) Place approximately 3 tablespoons of dough into the center of each husk, and fold to form tamales.

COOKING THE TAMALES:

(1) Add hot water to large pot with steamer basket lined with small husks.
(2) Cover tamales with remaining husks, and cover pot with lid.
(3) Steam tamales for 1 ¼ hours.
(4) To check for doneness, unwrap tamale. If done, dough will come off easily from husk. If dough sticks, rewrap and steam 15 to 20 more minutes.
(5) Serve warm and enjoy!

Mama's Chicken

SERVES 8-10

This dish is all about good home-style cooking. There's a little bit of my mom, my mother-in-law, and Louisiana wrapped up in it that makes it special for me. The mushrooms, wine, and Dijon come together to make an earthy comfort-food quality. We usually serve it for our Sunday brunch. At first, I had intended to have a regular chicken casserole dish for each brunch that we would call Mama's Chicken, with the goal of changing the casserole from week to week. But the first week we tried to change it, we caught a lot of flack from our customers, so we serve this now every week. *Note: We suggest using boneless chicken thighs, as opposed to breast meat, for a richer flavor.*

INGREDIENTS	MEASURE	CUT	PREPARATION
Chicken, thigh meat Kosher salt Black pepper	2 pounds 1 tablespoon 1 tablespoon		(1) Preheat oven to 375 degrees. (2) Season chicken with salt and pepper, and roast for approximately 30 minutes. Slice in half and reserve for final step.
Onions Garlic Butter	1 cup 2 tablespoons ¼ pound	Chopped Chopped	(3) In heavy-duty pot, sauté onions and garlic in butter.
Dijon mustard	¼ cup		(4) Add Dijon and fry for 3 minutes.
White wine Chicken broth (boxed is fine) Heavy cream	½ cup 1 cup 2 cups		(5) Add wine, broth, and cream, and cook 10 minutes.
Mushrooms	4 cups	Chopped	(6) Add mushrooms, and cook 10 minutes.
Rosemary, fresh Thyme, fresh	1 tablespoon 1 tablespoon	Chopped Chopped	(7) Add herbs and roasted chicken with juices to pot, and cook 10 minutes.

Pumpkin Bread

Pumpkin Bread

SERVES 8-10

This is one of the most popular recipes for pumpkins in the fall. If we're not treating the pumpkin like a squash for something savory, we do pies, flan, empanadas, or pumpkin bread. Just take a good coffeecake recipe, and add pumpkin to it. It turns a nice burnt orange, and we top it with streusel as well. Pumpkin bread is a beautiful addition to a breakfast spread.

INGREDIENTS	MEASURE	CUT		PREPARATION
Butter, chilled	4 tablespoons	Chopped into chunks		(1) For streusel topping, in large bowl using two forks, mix and mash up butter with sugars and flour until crumbly and loose, and set aside.
Sugar	1/4 cup			
Brown sugar	1/4 cup			
Flour	1 cup			
Pumpkin	1 cup	Roasted and puréed		(2) Preheat oven to 350 degrees, and prepare 9-inch-round cake pan with cooking spray. (3) In stand mixer, combine thoroughly pumpkin, sugar, oil, water, and eggs.
Sugar	1 1/4 cup			
Vegetable oil, preferably canola	1/2 cup			
Water	3 tablespoons			
Eggs	2			
All-purpose flour	1 3/4 cups		*Bread is done when it springs back when touched lightly. If not done, bake 5 minutes and check again.*	(4) In bowl, whisk together flour, spices, salt, and baking powder, and add to pumpkin mixture, mixing until just combined; don't overmix. (5) Stir in pecans. (6) Top with streusel, bake for 40 minutes, and cool slightly before removing from pan.
Cinnamon	1 teaspoon	Ground		
Ginger	1/2 teaspoon			
Nutmeg	1/2 teaspoon			
Salt	1 teaspoon			
Baking powder	1 tablespoon			
Pecans, Texas	1/2 cup	Chopped		

Bourbon Pecan Apple Cobbler

SERVES 8-10

This makes a soulful dessert for the season. Pecans, bourbon, and apples just naturally go well together. The key is to use something like a Granny Smith apple, which will hold up better in the baking. Other apples can get mealy and mushy. The tartness from the green apple dissipates with the addition of the other ingredients.

INGREDIENTS	MEASURE	CUT	PREPARATION
Apples, green	8 to 10	Peeled, cored, and sliced into ¼-inch pieces	(1) Preheat oven to 350 degrees, and spray a 10- or 12-inch-round cast-iron skillet with cooking spray or rub with oil. (2) Toss apples with sugar, spices, vanilla, and liquor.
Brown sugar	¾ cup		
Cinnamon	1 teaspoon		
Nutmeg	¼ teaspoon		
Vanilla	1 teaspoon		
Bourbon or Texas whiskey	2 tablespoons		
Pecans, Texas	1 cup	Chopped or whole	(3) Place apples in skillet, top evenly with pecans, and set aside.
Butter, chilled	8 ounces	Cut into pieces	(4) For streusel topping, in large bowl using two forks, mix and mash up butter with sugars and flour until crumbly and loose, then pour over apples. (5) Bake for approximately 45 minutes until evenly browned, and serve warm, with vanilla ice cream.
Sugar	1 cup		
Brown sugar	1 cup		
All-purpose flour	3 cups		

Pear, Ricotta, and Pecan Tart

Tarts

To me, tarts take the decadence of a good pie and put it into a more approachable size. It's thinner by nature of the baking tin you use, and you can't overstuff it. I always feel like it's not as much of an indulgence—unless I help myself to another serving. It's got to have a good crust and a really nice filling. Our pastry chef, Dee-Dee, uses a whole range of things, from traditional pie or graham cracker crusts to cheese or jelly fillings. In the fall, goat cheese and pumpkin are so good together. It's got both a savory and sweet quality, just like a good cheesecake. Roasted pear with goat cheese and pecans also works really well, and it looks amazing on the plate.

Pear, Ricotta, and Pecan Tart

SERVES 8-10

INGREDIENTS	MEASURE	CUT	PREPARATION
Graham cracker crumbs Pecans Butter, melted Sugar	1 cup ¼ cup 2 ounces 1 tablespoon	 Ground	(1) Preheat oven to 350 degrees. **For crust:** (2) Prepare 9-inch springform pan with cooking spray. (3) In bowl, combine crumbs, ground pecans, butter, and sugar. (4) Press into bottom of pan, cook for 5 minutes, and allow to cool.
Cream cheese Ricotta cheese Sugar Eggs, farm fresh	12 ounces 6 ounces ⅔ cup 3	Softened	**For ricotta filling:** (5) In stand mixer, whip together cheeses until no lumps remain, approximately 5 minutes. (6) Add sugar, and mix 1 minute. (7) Add eggs one at a time, scraping side of bowl with rubber spatula between eggs. (8) When no lumps remain, pour into crust.
Pears Pecan halves	3 1 cup	Peeled, cored, and sliced	(9) Place pears on top close together in one layer. (10) Arrange pecans on top, and bake until center is set, approximately 40 minutes. Refrigerate in pan for 4 hours before serving.

Pumpkin Goat Cheese Tart

SERVES 8-10

INGREDIENTS	MEASURE	CUT	PREPARATION
			(1) Preheat oven to 350 degrees.
Graham cracker crumbs	1 cup		**For crust:**
Pecans	¼ cup	Ground	(2) Prepare 9-inch springform pan with cooking spray. (3) In bowl, combine crumbs, ground pecans, butter, and sugar. (4) Press into bottom of pan, cook for 5 minutes, and allow to cool.
Butter, melted	2 ounces		
Sugar	1 tablespoon		
Cream cheese	8 ounces	Softened	**For goat cheese filling:**
Goat cheese	3 ounces		(5) In stand mixer whip together cheeses until no lumps remain, approximately 5 minutes. (6) Add sugar, and mix 1 minute. (7) Add eggs one at a time, scraping side of bowl with rubber spatula between eggs. (8) When no lumps remain, pour into crust.
Sugar	⅓ cup		
Eggs, farm fresh	2		
Roasted pumpkin purée	1 ½ cups		**For pumpkin filling:**
Sour cream	½ cup		(9) For pumpkin filling, in medium-sized bowl whisk together pumpkin purée and remaining ingredients until thoroughly combined and smooth, with no lumps. (10) Spoon over goat cheese filling and spread evenly; it's okay if goat cheese filling shows through. (11) Bake until center is set, approximately 40 minutes. Refrigerate in pan for 4 hours before serving.
Brown sugar	⅓ cup		
Egg, farm fresh	1		
Cinnamon	½ teaspoon		
Ginger	½ teaspoon		
Nutmeg	¼ teaspoon		
Salt	¼ teaspoon		

PEARS can be tricky because they tend to be too hard or overripe. The best way to handle pears is to buy them before they're ripe and then put them in a dark room. Sometimes they get a little black on the outsides but that's okay. Just cut that off and eat the rest. They're sweet and delicious.

We buy most of our pears from Lightsey Farms in Mexia when they're in season. We use them for our Fancy Chicken Salad and only cut them to order to keep them as pretty as possible on the salad. We also poach pears for desserts and make tarts and jams.

Pickles

This is another example of how you can preserve ingredients from every season. And you don't have to eat these plain. Adding a couple of pickled items to any entrée adds a little brightness to the flavor profile, especially if there's already a heaviness to the dish. Beets, fennel, radishes, carrots. These are all ingredients that preserve well when they're pickled, and they contribute that snappy bite to fall dishes.

Pickled Beets

(MAKES 3-4 MASON JARS)

INGREDIENTS	MEASURE	CUT	PREPARATION
Red wine vinegar Water Pickling spice Dried chiles Sugar	1 cup 2 cups ¼ cup 3 ¼ cup		(1) In large pot, boil together vinegar and next 4 ingredients, strain, and set liquid aside.
Beets, your favorite Kosher salt	1 pound 1 tablespoon		(2) In another pot, add beets and salt, cover with water, and cook until fork-tender, approximately 40 minutes. (3) Drain, let rest 10 minutes, peel (should peel easily), and slice into bite-size pieces.
Fennel seeds Caraway seeds Mustard seeds Coriander seeds Cumin seeds	1 teaspoon 1 teaspoon 1 teaspoon 1 teaspoon 1 teaspoon		(4) In skillet on stovetop, combine seeds and roast until aromatic, 4 to 5 minutes. (5) Allow to cool, and grind in coffee grinder. (6) In bowl, pour pickling liquid over beets to cover, add ground seeds, and leave at room temperature for 2 to 4 hours. (7) Place in jars, then refrigerate.

Pickled Fennel

(MAKES 3-4 MASON JARS)

INGREDIENTS	MEASURE	CUT	PREPARATION
Champagne vinegar Water Pickling spice Dried chiles Sugar	1 cup 2 cups 1/4 cup 3 1/4 cup		(1) In large pot, boil together vinegar and next 4 ingredients, strain, and set liquid aside.
Fennel	1/2 pound	Thinly sliced	(2) In bowl, pour pickling liquid over fennel to cover and leave at room temperature for 2 to 4 hours. (3) Place in jars, then refrigerate.

Pickled Radishes

(MAKES 3-4 MASON JARS)

INGREDIENTS	MEASURE	CUT	PREPARATION
White vinegar Water Pickling spice Dried chiles	1 cup 2 cups 1/4 cup 3		(1) In large pot, boil together vinegar and next 3 ingredients, strain, and set liquid aside.
Radishes	1/2 pound	Sliced	(2) In bowl, pour pickling liquid over radishes to cover and leave at room temperature for 2 to 4 hours. (3) Place in jars, then refrigerate.

Pickled Carrots

(MAKES 3-4 MASON JARS)

INGREDIENTS	MEASURE	CUT	PREPARATION
White vinegar Water Pickling spice Dried chiles	1 cup 2 cups 1/4 cup 3		(1) In large pot, boil together vinegar and next 3 ingredients, strain, and set liquid aside.
Carrots	1/2 pound	Peeled and julienned	(2) In bowl, pour pickling liquid over carrots to cover and leave at room temperature for 2 to 4 hours. (3) Place in jars, then refrigerate.

WINTER

Pomegranate Sage Rita

Bourbon Smash

Pomegranate Sage Rita

MAKES 4-6

We like to create cocktails that are easy to make with fresh ingredients that unite different seasonal flavors. The pomegranate and sage worked so well with the tequila that this cocktail has been on our menu from the beginning. We've tried this drink with a lot of different tequilas, but the 1800 Silver works best. Use a different tequila if you like, but it does change the flavor profile.

INGREDIENTS	MEASURE	CUT	PREPARATION
POM Wonderful 100 percent pomegranate juice Lime juice Simple syrup *(see page 18)*	4 ounces 4 ounces 4 ounces	 Fresh squeezed	**For Pomegranate Rita Mix:** (1) In large container combine juices and syrup.
1800 Silver tequila Cointreau	8 ounces 4 ounces		(2) In pitcher or carafe of your choice, combine Pomegranate Rita Mix with tequila and Cointreau.
Sage leaves	12		(3) Add 6 to 8 sage leaves, stir, and allow mixture to steep 5 to 10 minutes. (4) Stir, pour over ice in glasses, and garnish with sage leaves.

Bourbon Smash

MAKES 4-6

This is our take on an Old Fashioned. We wanted a citrusy bourbon drink, so we muddle together simple syrup, bitters, and oranges. Then we add Paula's Texas Orange and bourbon. It has a nice citrus flavor, perfect in the winter. If you can't find Paula's Texas Orange, grab triple sec, Grand Marnier, or Cointreau.

INGREDIENTS	MEASURE	CUT	PREPARATION
Orange Maker's Mark bourbon Paula's Texas Orange liqueur Simple syrup *(see page 18)* Ice	1 9 ounces 3 ounces 3 ounces 2 scoops	Cut into 12 wedges	(1) In large container, squeeze and drop wedges and add next 4 ingredients. (2) Stir thoroughly and fill glasses ¾ full.
Angostura aromatic bitters Soda water Maraschino cherries	6 dashes Splash For garnish		(3) Add 1 or 2 dashes bitters, splash with soda, and finish with cherry.

Dad's Holiday Whiskey Sour

MAKES 4-6

There wasn't a lot of drinking in my house when I was growing up, but once the holidays rolled around, that meant Thanksgiving dinners and Christmas buffets. All the guests were greeted with a whiskey sour, and a bottle of Lambrusco was always on the table. I will gladly forget the Lambrusco, but the whiskey sours were pretty tasty and always remind me of the flavor of the holidays. This is an easy recipe, made up by my dad, Ralph Kamm. I served the drinks one recent Christmas, and everyone enjoyed the tart and sweet mixture before dinner. –*As remembered by Tom Kamm*

INGREDIENTS	MEASURE	CUT		PREPARATION
Frozen lemonade	6 ounces			(1) In blender, combine all ingredients except garnishes until egg white is foamy and ice is slightly chunky.
Bourbon whiskey	6 ounces		**I like Buffalo Trace.*	
Water	6 ounces			
Ice cubes	6 ounces			
Egg white	1			
Angostura bitters	Dash for optional garnish			(2) Pour into champagne glasses, dash with bitters, and top with cherry.
Maraschino cherries	For garnish			

Bourbon Milk Punch

MAKES 4-6

We were inspired for this on a trip to New Orleans after having it from a soft-serve machine in a bar. It was fantastic. It has this great holiday flavor and a wonderful texture to it, between a punch and a shake, and it goes down good.

INGREDIENTS	MEASURE	CUT		PREPARATION
Bourbon of choice Milk, whole Vanilla extract Simple syrup or powdered sugar Ice Jack Allen's Kitchen homemade Eggnog Ice Cream *(see page 303)*	1 cup 2 cups 1 tablespoon ½ cup 1 small scoop 3 large scoops			(1) In blender, combine all ingredients except nutmeg for 30 seconds.
Nutmeg	Pinch			(2) Pour into 10-ounce glasses, garnish with nutmeg, and serve with straws.

Pumpkin Spice Butter Rum

MAKES 1

A traditional holiday cocktail that you don't see as much anymore, hot-buttered rum needed a comeback with a little touch of Jack Allen's. I did it, once again with the help of Treaty Oak Distilling's Barrel Reserve Rum, an aged rum. And we don't use just any butter; we use Pumpkin Spice Butter. It's a comforting after-dinner drink for the holiday season, or just sip it to warm up on those eight cold days each year we have here in Texas!

INGREDIENTS	MEASURE	CUT		PREPARATION
Water				(1) Set water to boil.
Caramel, melted			**Additional garnish: Red bow on mug handle.*	(2) For garnish, dip rim of footed mug to coat in caramel.
JAK's Pumpkin Spice Butter *(opposite)* Treaty Oak Barrel Reserve Rum	2 tablespoons 2 ounces			(3) Add butter to mug and pour in rum to reach halfway in glass. (4) Pour in boiling water to fill, stir, and serve.

PUMPKIN SPICE BUTTER (MAKES 1½ CUPS)

INGREDIENTS	MEASURE	CUT	PREPARATION
Butter	2 sticks (or 8 ounces)	Softened	(1) In mixing bowl, using handheld mixer, blend all ingredients well.
Pumpkin purée	2 tablespoons		
Cinnamon	1 teaspoon		
Nutmeg	¼ teaspoon		
Brown sugar	2 tablespoons		

American Oak
24 Month
Medium Plus Toast

05 C-1
Shiraz
2220
05 CS
AZ
0235
05 CS
AZ
0232
2148
05 CS
A-2
0382
05 CS
A-2
2227
8039
0402
0391
05 CS
AZ
0397
2239
2258

TEXAS WINE

AS TOLD BY TOM KAMM

FOLKS MOVE HERE all the time from places like California, and I love when they are at the bar, looking for a wine to try. They turn their nose up when I suggest a Texas wine, but I say, "Please, humor me, sample a few of them." Most of the time they are game, and when they taste, they are shocked. They cannot believe it's Texas fruit, and they cannot believe how great it is. Now, that's exciting. And that's why we stand by the Texas wines we sell. At the rate we are going, the future will only get better.

Ten years ago, we would not have considered putting Texas wine on our list. Although Texas wine has a long history, it has not always been a great story—especially in the glass.

Spanish missionaries planted the first vineyards here in the 1600s, but winemaking in Texas didn't really take root until the mid-1970s. Following California's foray onto the global wine scene, a few pioneering spirits, including Clinton "Doc" McPherson of Llano Estacado Winery, Paul Bonarrigo of Messina Hof Winery, and Ed Auler of Fall Creek Vineyards, made a go of growing wine grapes in the Texas climate. At the time, California's success with varieties such as Merlot, Cabernet Sauvignon, and Chardonnay tempted Texans to try their hand with the same. Besides a few highlights throughout the 1980s and 1990s, with wineries such as Becker Vineyards and Inwood Estates Vineyards joining the scene, the quality of Texas wine was generally unremarkable.

But a lot has changed in the past few years. Now we have winemakers and grape growers using grapes like Viognier, Tempranillo, Mourvedre, and Sangiovese that are from warm-climate regions like southern France, Spain, and Italy. Those grapes just make more sense for Texas.

The overall quality of the grapes grown in the High Plains and the Hill Country has also gotten better, as has the caliber of winemakers who are making the right decisions in the vineyard and in the winery. Now new and promising Texas wine producers are bringing their wine to us to try, and I have to say I've been pretty impressed.

I think the entire industry has made great progress in the past decade. Wineries like William Chris Vineyards, Pedernales Cellars, and Duchman Family Winery are making nice wines. McPherson Cellars out of Lubbock is one of the most consistent, and usually at a good price point.

BUT BACK TO THE older wineries, like Messina Hof, Fall Creek Vineyards, Llano Estacado Winery, Becker Vineyards, and Flat Creek Estates Winery. They had the hardest job: figuring out what would work in Texas. They were trying to build a brand when very few people would listen. Those guys plowed the ground for newer producers. Then, over the years, they evolved with the industry, so we're happy to put a number of their wines on our list as well.

In some cases, price point is still an issue. A lot of great Texas wines are priced higher than we can sell, in relation to other wines we carry. But as more wineries hear about our willingness to promote what the state produces, they become willing to work with us on price so that we can get their wines out there.

Still, it has been a challenge to change our guests' perception of Texas wine. In general, they are more accustomed to wines using familiar grapes, like Chardonnay and Merlot. But Texas is better with grapes like Viognier, Tempranillo, and Mourvedre—all of which are hard enough to pronounce let alone recognizable by our customers.

But honestly, it's a challenge we welcome. We work closely with our staff and educate them on the producers, the grapes, and how the wines taste. That way, they can transfer that knowledge to our guests and invite them to try something new. That's how you change perception.

MIDDLE ROW, RIGHT PHOTO BY JESSICA DUPUY

Broccoli Casserole

Grilled Veggies

Cauliflower Couscous

JAK's Slaw

JAK's Slaw

SERVES 6-8

This is a great slaw because it's spicy, sweet, and crunchy. We use Baja Dressing, made up of equal parts Mango Citrus Dressing *(see page 282)*, with red chiles and mangos, and Jalapeño Tartar Sauce. We're after texture for this, which comes from cabbage and carrots. You don't want a mushy slaw. So we toss every serving of JAK's Slaw to order, in a salad bowl with tongs. It just keeps the texture vibrant and crisp.

INGREDIENTS	MEASURE	CUT	PREPARATION
Cabbage, green	1 quart	Julienned	(1) In large stainless-steel bowl, combine vegetables well.
Cabbage, red	1 quart	Julienned	
Jicama	1 quart	Peeled; julienned	
Carrots	1 quart	Peeled, with stem and tips removed; julienned	
Cilantro	1 cup, packed	Rough chopped	
Baja Dressing	1 cup		**For Baja Dressing:** (2) Combine ½ cup Mango Citrus Dressing *(see page 282)* and ½ cup Jalapeño Tartar Sauce *(below)*. (3) Toss well with slaw, and serve immediately.

JALAPEÑO TARTAR SAUCE (MAKES 2 CUPS)

INGREDIENTS	MEASURE	CUT	PREPARATION
Onion	¼ cup	Chopped	(1) In food processor, blend all ingredients together well.
Cilantro	½ cup	Chopped	
Jalapeños, fresh	¼ cup	Diced	
White vinegar	2 tablespoons		
Dijon mustard	3 tablespoons		
Mayonnaise	1 cup		
Chipotle	1 tablespoon		

CABBAGE We can get cabbage in Texas. We get most of it from Two Happy Children Farm, as well as a few other farms. We'll also get some great bok choy cabbage from Amador Farms. We use it mainly for JAK's Slaw, but sometimes we'll do soups with it and sides, like kimchi and sauerkraut. People don't always love just cabbage as a side. Personally, I could eat it all day long, but you never know, so we use it in moderation with other dishes.

Cauliflower Couscous

SERVES 6-8

This is a lot simpler than it sounds. Anytime you chop cauliflower, you end up with all these tiny little bits left behind. To me it looks like couscous. So we decided to just shave the whole thing, add some olive oil, salt, and pepper, and serve it as a side like couscous. We don't even cook it but just let it marinate for a few hours to meld the flavors. It's delicious and really healthy for you.

INGREDIENTS	MEASURE	CUT	PREPARATION
Cauliflower	1 head	Shaved to the size of uncooked rice	(1) Mix together all ingredients, and let stand at least 5 hours before using.
Olive oil	3/4 cup		
Sherry vinegar	1/4 cup		
Green onion	1/2 cup	Chopped, green and white parts	
Black olives	3/4 cup	Chopped	
Capers	1/4 cup		
Red pepper, roasted	1/2 cup	Chopped (store-bought is fine)	
Feta cheese crumbles	1 cup		
Salt and pepper	To taste		

Potato Casserole

SERVES 6-8

This casserole is always a crowd pleaser. We use our Chunky Potato Mashers, which are Idaho russet and red potatoes, and we leave them chunky. We add Pimiento Cheese, put it in a casserole dish, top it with gratin, and bake it. It's the perfect creamy side for our steaks.

INGREDIENTS	MEASURE	CUT	PREPARATION
Chunky Potato Mashers *(see page 279)*	2/3 part		(1) Preheat oven to 400 degrees. (2) In mixing bowl, combine potatoes and cheese.
Pimiento Cheese *(see page 109)*	1/3 part		
Panko breadcrumbs	2 cups		(4) For gratin, combine breadcrumbs and Parmesan. (3) Place potato mixture in buttered casserole dish, top with gratin, and bake 35 to 40 minutes, until golden brown.
Parmesan cheese	2 cups	Grated	

Roasted Garlic

MAKES 1½ CUPS

The cool thing about garlic is that after you roast it, it gets creamy and becomes a whole new ingredient. Roasting makes the flavor milder compared with straight garlic, which can be a little sharp and spicy—still a choice option for certain dishes. If you're going to put the time into roasting some, do a few cups. Then jar it in a good olive oil, and it should last a few weeks refrigerated. You can use it with anything, from dressings and mashed potatoes to steaks or chicken right off the grill, or even on a good bread for garlic toast.

INGREDIENTS	MEASURE	CUT		PREPARATION
Garlic cloves	4 cups	Peeled and cleaned	**Garlic can be refrigerated and used for up to 4 weeks.*	(1) Preheat oven to 375. (2) Stack garlic in small casserole dish slightly covered with water. (3) Bake approximately 45 minutes.
Water	To cover			

Green Garlic Ash

SERVES 6

Kris Olsen, from Milagro Farms, turned me on to green garlic. We use it sparingly, but it shows up in our soups a lot. We also make an ash with it, which imparts a little more flavor to something like a scallop or shrimp dish for a special event. Or you can use it to make an emulsification for an oil and slather it on French fries. You won't be able to kiss anyone for a week, but who cares.

INGREDIENTS	MEASURE	CUT	PREPARATION
Green garlic sprigs	24	Trimmed	(1) Coat sprigs with oil. (2) On prepared grill, slightly char sprigs until gray. (3) Remove from grill and place so not touching on baking sheet.
Olive oil	¼ cup		

GARLIC We get a lot of our garlic from Tecalote Farm. Garlic grows really well here in Texas, and if you store it in a cool place, you can have it all year. Between garlic and onions, it's hard to make any savory dish without at least one of them adding to the overall flavor. When you are buying garlic, squeeze the whole bulb. It should feel firm and plump. I like getting the ones with the larger cloves, because the small ones are a pain to peel.

GREEN GARLIC is just an early version of garlic, before the cloves on the bulb have had a chance to form. It's often associated with spring, but in Texas we start to see it in the later part of winter. Green garlic is best in simple preparations that allow its flavor to show through. Try it with scrambled eggs, mashed potatoes, soups, grilled asparagus, and fresh peas.

Grilled Brussels Sprouts

SERVES 4-6

If you're trying to change someone's bad opinion of Brussels sprouts, give this recipe a try. When you put them on the grill, the water that's still caught inside the little cabbage heads will steam through while they're cooking, which helps soften and cook them. I recommend a perforated grill pan, and use it like you're stir-frying sprouts on the grill.

INGREDIENTS	MEASURE	CUT	PREPARATION
Brussels sprouts	2 pints	Outer leaves removed	(1) In saucepan, cover Brussels sprouts with water, add salt, and bring to boil; remove immediately and strain.
Salt	1 tablespoon		
Olive oil	1/4 cup		(2) In stainless-steel bowl, combine oil, onion, and seasonings with Brussels sprouts. (3) On prepared grill, grill until completely charred, turning for even cooking.
Onion	1	Quartered	
Black pepper	1/2 tablespoon		
Kosher salt	1/2 tablespoon		
Dijon mustard	1/4 cup		(4) For Dijon vinaigrette, in stainless-steel bowl, whisk together mustard, vinegar, and oil. (5) Add Brussels sprouts, and toss. (6) To serve, place on platter and drizzle with Balsamic Syrup *(see page 309)*.
Sherry vinegar	2 tablespoons		
Olive oil	2 tablespoons		

BRUSSELS SPROUTS I was one of those crazy kids who liked Brussels sprouts. My mom just opened up a can and served it. I wasn't exposed to fresh Brussels sprouts until about a decade ago in Austin. I was walking through Whole Foods and saw them. I'd never seen them just sitting in a bag. I knew what to do with them, but I had never thought about grilling, roasting, or frying them until I saw my son Bryce do it. I think it hit a trend on menus that got a little out of hand, but I'll tell you what. A lot of people are eating them who would never touch them before.

Caramelized Onion Sauce

MAKES APPROXIMATELY 2 ½ QUARTS

We use this as a sauce for steak and in a gravy for meatloaf. Many people don't realize onions are naturally sweet. They're full of sugar. To caramelize them, you chop them really well and cook them low and slow with a little bit of olive oil. You want them to get really brown and golden. And when you add broth or wine, it pretty much dissolves but leaves so much flavor. If you cook the sauce right, it looks like a good demi-glace. The key is not to rush it or walk away from it for too long. You have to be on top of the stove and have at least 2 hours to do it.

INGREDIENTS	MEASURE	CUT		PREPARATION
Onions, white Vegetable oil	2 pounds ¼ cup	Julienned	**Look for deep brown color but not burnt.*	(1) In large skillet or braising pan on low, caramelize onions in oil for 1 ½ hours, stirring every 5 minutes.
Apple cider vinegar	⅓ cup			(2) Deglaze with vinegar for approximately 3 minutes, then using hand-held mixer purée.
Beef broth (boxed is fine)	3 quarts, boxed			(3) Return to skillet, add broth, and simmer for approximately 30 minutes, skimming as needed.
Honey	½ cup			(4) Add honey, and simmer for approximately 20 minutes.
Cornstarch Water	3 tablespoons 3 tablespoons			(5) In small bowl, make cornstarch slurry, stir into pot, and cook 5 minutes.
Salt and pepper	To taste		**Sauce can be frozen in small batches.*	(6) Season to taste.

ONION is everywhere. I feel sorry for the person who comes in here and says he can't eat onions. I mean, it's just flavor. Maybe the one place it doesn't show up is the JAK's Slaw. The raw onion is just too strong. We use raw onion only for a burger or pico de gallo. But, really, it's in all of our soups, stews, tacos, everything.

Short Ribs

SERVES 4-6

You can't beat short ribs as a hearty dish when it's cold outside. It's basically an elegant form of pot roast, with a much richer flavor, which comes from the bones. The key is letting it cook long enough. If you cook it right, it's one of the best parts of the cow. If you don't cook it right, it's one of the worst cuts of meat you'll eat, tough and sinewy. Sear it for good brown color on all sides. Then add liquids and flavorings to it. You'll know it's ready when the bones poke out and the meat starts to fall away. For gravy, use everything left in the pan. Mash all the vegetables, using a potato masher, with some of the braising liquid. You can use some potato or cornstarch to thicken it up if you like. Serve over Chunky Potato Mashers *(see page 279)* or Cheesy Grits *(see page 278)* with a big pour of gravy, and you'll be in heaven.

INGREDIENTS	MEASURE	CUT		PREPARATION
Short ribs, bone in	5 to 6 pounds	Cut apart between each bone		(1) In mixing bowl, season ribs evenly.
Kosher salt	2 tablespoons			
Black pepper	2 tablespoons			
Olive oil	¼ cup		**Can be done in batches then use same pot after browning.*	(2) In pot large enough to accommodate all ingredients, bring oil to high heat and brown ribs, 2 to 3 minutes per side; do not overcrowd. (3) Preheat oven to 350 degrees.
Ancho chiles	3	Chopped		(4) In food processor, combine chiles with next 6 ingredients until smooth. (5) Add to pot with meat, and cook, stirring often, for 15 minutes, scraping the bottom for all the goodness.
Onion	1 ½ cup	Chopped		
Celery	2 ribs	Peeled and chopped		
Carrots	1 cup	Chopped		
Garlic	¼ cup			
Tomato paste	1 cup			
Red wine (your favorite leftover wine)	3 cups			
Thyme	5 sprigs		**Number 7 is a kitchen trick, but use a lid if you have one.*	(6) Tie herbs in pouch and add to pot with water. (7) Double wrap pot with plastic wrap, place foil on top to completely seal, and cook in oven for approximately 40 minutes. (8) Remove, stir, check for doneness, rewrap, and cook for 30 to 40 minutes, until meat is fork tender and bone is slightly falling off.
Rosemary	2 sprigs			
Bay leaves	2			
Water	3 cups			
Salt and pepper	To taste			9) Season to taste.

Cheesy Grits

SERVES 4-6

Here is a real homey Southern staple. You can serve grits on their own, but in my opinion they need something else. You could add butter and cream, but when you add cheese to the mix, it adds a depth of flavor. We use cheddar and Monterey Jack, but play around with different cheeses to suit what you're serving. The cool thing about grits is they are a good canvas for anything, chicken, shrimp, pork, steak. You can't really go wrong with this side dish. If you have leftovers, pull them out of the fridge the next day, cube them up, fry them in a skillet as grit cakes, and serve them with a couple of fried eggs.

INGREDIENTS	MEASURE	CUT	PREPARATION
Chicken broth (boxed is fine)	4 cups		(1) In medium saucepan, bring chicken broth to a boil.
Grits, not instant Garlic	1 cup 1 tablespoon	 Chopped	(2) Slowly whisk in grits and garlic. (3) Reduce heat to low, and cook, stirring every 2 minutes, until smooth and not gritty; 30 to 40 minutes should do it.
Cheese, your choice *(try Pimiento Cheese, page 109)* Butter Salt and pepper	1 cup 4 tablespoons To taste	 Cubed 	(4) Add cheese and butter to grits, mix well, and season to taste.

Chunky Potato Mashers

SERVES 6-8

It's too hard to do real whipped potatoes at a high volume, and I've always liked chunkier mashed potatoes anyway. We use Idaho russet and red potatoes for our mashers, because of the texture. You have to cook the red potatoes cut bigger and the russet potatoes cut smaller to get the right consistency. And you always peel the russets but not the reds. Russets are unpredictable, and the skins can make it a little starchy. I like having the little bits of red potato skin in there though. It gives it a rustic feel and adds to the texture.

INGREDIENTS	MEASURE	CUT	PREPARATION
Idaho russet potatoes	2 pounds	Peeled and cut smaller than red potatoes for even cooking	(1) In large stockpot, cover potatoes with water and boil approximately 30 minutes, until fork tender; drain through colander immediately.
Red potatoes	1 pound	Cut in half	
Butter	¼ pound		(2) Using handheld masher, mix in butter, sour cream, and Roasted Garlic, mashing to chunky consistency, 2 to 3 minutes.
Sour cream	¼ pound		
Roasted Garlic *(see page 273)*	¼ cup		
Salt and pepper	To taste		(3) Season to taste.

Fish Caldo

MAKES 8-10

What better way to use your fresh catch from a day of fishing, especially if the day was a cold one? This is a good base for any kind of seafood soup. You could use shrimp, oysters, and any kind of fish. The only tip is to put your fish in first and your shrimp or oysters in toward the end, because the latter can get tough if they are overcooked. The fish will just flake part, which doesn't matter as much. The flavors in this stew are rich in depth and luscious from the fresh fish.

INGREDIENTS	MEASURE	CUT	PREPARATION
Roasted Garlic *(see page 273)*	1/4 cup	Mashed	(1) In oversize stockpot, bring all ingredients except fish to boil, then simmer.
Seafood stock *(below)*	3 quarts		
Tomatoes	15 ounces, or 1 can	Diced	
Potatoes, russet	2 cups	Peeled, 1/4-inch diced	
Corn, fresh	1 cup	Kernels removed from cob	
Onion	2 cups	Chopped	
Green bell pepper	1/2 cup	Chopped	
Jalapeño	2 tablespoons	Seeded and diced	
Fish, mild, such as redfish, black drum, or flounder	2 pounds	Rough chopped	(2) Add fish and simmer approximately 30 minutes.
Cilantro and onion	For garnish	Chopped	(3) Garnish and serve with Veggie Studded Rice *(see page 227)*.
Onion wedges	For garnish	Diced	
Limes	For garnish	Cut in wedges	

SEAFOOD STOCK (MAKES AS MUCH AS YOU TOSS IN)

INGREDIENTS	MEASURE	CUT	PREPARATION
Fish scraps			(1) In stockpot, cover with water and bring to boil, then simmer for approximately 30 minutes. (2) Using colander, strain and reserve liquid.
Shrimp shells			
Onion	1	Chopped	
Bay leaves	5		

South Texas Tacos

I have always liked street food, from growing up in the Valley and visiting Mexico. And so we wanted to do something like the tacos you get in a simple food truck on the street, with chicken, beef, pork, and shrimp. You need all the other components too: rice, beans, guacamole, pico de gallo, tortillas, and, of course, some lime to squeeze on there. What makes ours a little different is small tortillas, from our friends at Fiesta Tortillas. I want the taco to be 2 bites. With bigger tortillas, you're a few bites in and everything falls out. This is meant to be the perfect finger food, something you can build on your own while getting sticky fingers.

Baja Shrimp with Mango Citrus Dressing

SERVES 8-10

Here is one of the ways we spotlight Texas shrimp, which is just the best around. We like the 21/25 brown shrimp, so a customer gets 7 or 8 shrimp with the meal (about ⅓ pound). We use Mango Citrus Dressing, which we also use for our JAK's Slaw, and sauté it to give it a little heat. Then we finish it with a little cream for a really great taco.

INGREDIENTS	MEASURE	CUT	PREPARATION
Mangos	2	Peeled, pitted, and diced into ¼-inch pieces	**For Mango Citrus Dressing:** (1) In large stainless steel bowl combine mango and next 4 ingredients well.
Mint, fresh	2 tablespoons	Stemmed and chopped	
Green onions	¼ cup	Chopped	
Sweet chile sauce (find in Asian section of grocery store)	1 cup		
Orange juice	¼ cup		
Butter	2 tablespoons		**For shrimp:** (1) In saucepan on medium heat, melt butter. (2) Add shrimp and keep separated, slightly raise heat, and fry 2 to 3 minutes until almost done. (3) Add ¾ cup Mango Citrus Dressing and cook approximately 1 minute.
Shrimp	1 pound, medium sized	Peeled and deveined	
Heavy cream	½ cup		(4) Add cream, and cook until slightly thickened, 2 to 3 minutes.

Barbacoa

SERVES 8-10

Traditionally, Mexican barbacoa is made with cow head parts, like the cheeks, but we use a shoulder so it's easier on our guests. We roast it for about 6 hours with cilantro, red chiles, garlic, beer, and salt, and it just falls apart. We use it for our tacos but also for our Barbacoa Stackers, which are like cheesy nachos.

INGREDIENTS	MEASURE	CUT	PREPARATION
Beef chuck	4 pounds	Cut into 4-inch cubes	(1) Preheat oven to 325 degrees. (2) In large stainless-steel mixing bowl, combine all ingredients except water and beer.
Cilantro	1 cup, packed	Chopped	
Garlic	¼ cup	Chopped	
Yellow onion	2 cups	Chopped	
Red chile powder	1 tablespoon		
Oranges	2	Quartered	
Guajillo dried chiles (or your favorite)	4		
Water	2 cups		(3) In metal roasting pan, place mixture and add water and beer. (4) Seal pan well with lid or 2 layers plastic wrap covered with foil, and cook for 2 ½ to 3 hours; allow to cool. (5) Using tongs, shred beef and remove as much fat as possible. (6) Strain cooking liquid, skim off fat, and add liquid back to meat.
Beer, Lone Star, of course	1 can minus 1 sip for the cook		

Chicken Tinga

SERVES 8-10

Tinga is basically a smoky tomato sauce with onions and usually chipotle. You can do it with any sort of protein, but we use it with chicken for our street tacos. We grill the chicken first and then boil it to stew it down. Then we add tomatoes, onions, and peppers to it to make it tinga.

INGREDIENTS	MEASURE	CUT	PREPARATION
Roasted chicken	1 pound	Meat picked from bone	(1) In large saucepan, heat together all ingredients, and season to taste.
Adobo, from chipotle chiles	2 tablespoons		
Tomatoes	1 cup	Julienned	
Red onion	1 cup	Julienned	
Pico de Gallo *(see page 98)*	1 cup		
Salt and pepper	To taste		

Baja Shrimp with Mango Citrus Dressing

Veggie Studded Rice and Black Beans

Chicken Tinga

Green Chile Pork

Barbacoa

Green Chile Pork

SERVES 8-10

This is a traditional dish, sort of a lazy man's way of making carnitas, which take a lot of work. But you can stew this, add a bunch of green chiles and tomatillos, and let it cook for a few hours. The key is pork butt. Trim off some of the fat, but not much. Definitely don't use something lean like pork tenderloin. It's just too dry. You can make it as spicy as you want, and be sure you have tortillas, rice, beans, and guacamole. We let our meat cook down quite a bit, but you can easily make a stew out of it by just adding more broth.

INGREDIENTS	MEASURE	CUT	PREPARATION
Vegetable oil	¼ cup		(1) In braising pan on medium heat, bring oil to smoking.
Pork butt	4 pounds	Trimmed slightly and cut into 1 x ¼–inch pieces	(2) Using long-handled spoon, add pork. (3) Sauté until brown and juice evaporates, 30 to 35 minutes.
Tomatillos	1 pound	Washed and peeled	(4) In large stockpot on medium heat, add next 8 ingredients and boil for 3 minutes, then blend with immersion blender until smooth. (5) Add to pork pan, and simmer on medium for approximately 40 minutes.
Onion, white	2 cups	Quartered	
Garlic, fresh	2 tablespoons	Chopped	
Jalapeño	1	Chopped	
Water, warm-tap	3 cups		
Chicken broth (boxed is fine)	2 cups		
Cilantro	1 cup		
Lime juice	2 tablespoons		
Anaheim peppers	½ pound	Roasted, peeled, seeded, and julienned 1 to 2 inches long	(6) Add peppers to pork mixture, stir, and simmer for 2 minutes.

Venison Stew/Chili

SERVES 8-10

Use any kind of venison or even wild boar for this hearty winter dish. We like to work with Broken Arrow Ranch to see what kinds of venison we can get for this. It's a hunter's delight. The key to ours is chiles and beer.

INGREDIENTS	MEASURE	CUT		PREPARATION
Kosher salt	1 tablespoon			(1) For stew seasoning, in bowl mix together first 8 ingredients and set aside.
Black pepper	1 tablespoon			
Paprika	1 tablespoon			
Chili powder	1 tablespoon			
Garlic powder	1 tablespoon			
Onion powder	1 tablespoon			
Oregano	1 tablespoon	Ground		
Thyme	1 tablespoon	Ground		
Olive oil	3 tablespoons			(2) In large thick-bottom pot, heat oil on high.
Venison stew meat	2 pounds	¼-inch diced		(3) In bowl, toss venison with flour. (4) When oil is hot, cook venison 2 to 3 minutes, stirring occasionally.
Flour	¼ cup			
Onion	2 cups	Chopped		(5) Stir vegetables, tomatoes, bay leaves, and ½ stew seasoning to meat pot, and cook on high approximately 4 to 5 minutes, stirring occasionally.
Celery	1 cup	Chopped		
Carrots	1 cup	Chopped		
Tomatoes	15 ½ ounces, or 1 can	Diced		
Bay leaves	2			
Beer, your favorite	1 bottle or can		** Tortillas will thicken it up so you may need to add more broth.*	(6) Add last 3 ingredients, reduce to simmer, and cook approximately 1 hour, until meat is tender. Add more stew seasoning to taste or save it for next time.
Beef broth (boxed is fine)	4 cups			
Corn tortillas	6	Chopped		

Meatloaf with Wild Mushroom Gravy

SERVES 8-10

Meatloaf is just a home-style dish you can't escape. But it can be really good or really bad. I like to get a good mixture of ground chuck and ground pork. You need a ground chuck with about 20 percent fat. You don't want to go too lean or it gets dry. Turkey meatloaf is fine, but it's just dry—and kinda boring. Ours is real moist, and we kick it off with Creole mustard, Tabasco, Worcestershire, onions, and green garlic. We'll put ketchup on it, because you just have to, but the gravy we make really sets it off. The other thing is, cook it quick, at about 400 degrees, to get it crispy. It has to be a perfect loaf—about 4 inches across and 2 inches high. That way it gets just the right consistency.

INGREDIENTS	MEASURE	CUT	PREPARATION
Celery stalks	1 cup	Finely chopped	(1) Preheat oven to 375 degrees. (2) In large stainless-steel bowl, with hands thoroughly combine all ingredients up to and including ½ cup ketchup. (3) Form uniform loaf on baking pan, approximately 2 ½ inches high, leaving space around edges. (4) Drizzle 1 cup ketchup on meatloaf, and bake 25 to 30 minutes, until golden brown.
Bell peppers, red	¾ cup	Finely chopped	
Onion	¾ cup	Finely chopped	
Ground beef, extra lean	2 pounds		
Ground pork	1 pound		
Eggs	3		
Creole mustard	2 tablespoons		
Worcestershire sauce	1 tablespoon		
Roasted Garlic *(see page 273)*	2 tablespoons		
Cayenne pepper	1 teaspoon		
Kosher salt	1 tablespoon		
Breadcrumbs	1 ¼ cups		
Tabasco sauce	3 dashes		
Paprika	2 tablespoons		
Ketchup	½ cup, plus 1 cup		
Mushrooms, your favorite	3 cups	Diced into bite-size pieces	**For Wild Mushroom Gravy:** (5) In saucepan sauté mushrooms in butter until tender.
Butter	¼ cup		
Caramelized Onion Sauce *(see page 275)*	4 cups	**Serve meatloaf slices topped with gravy.*	(6) Add Caramelized Onion Sauce, and cook on medium heat approximately 5 minutes.

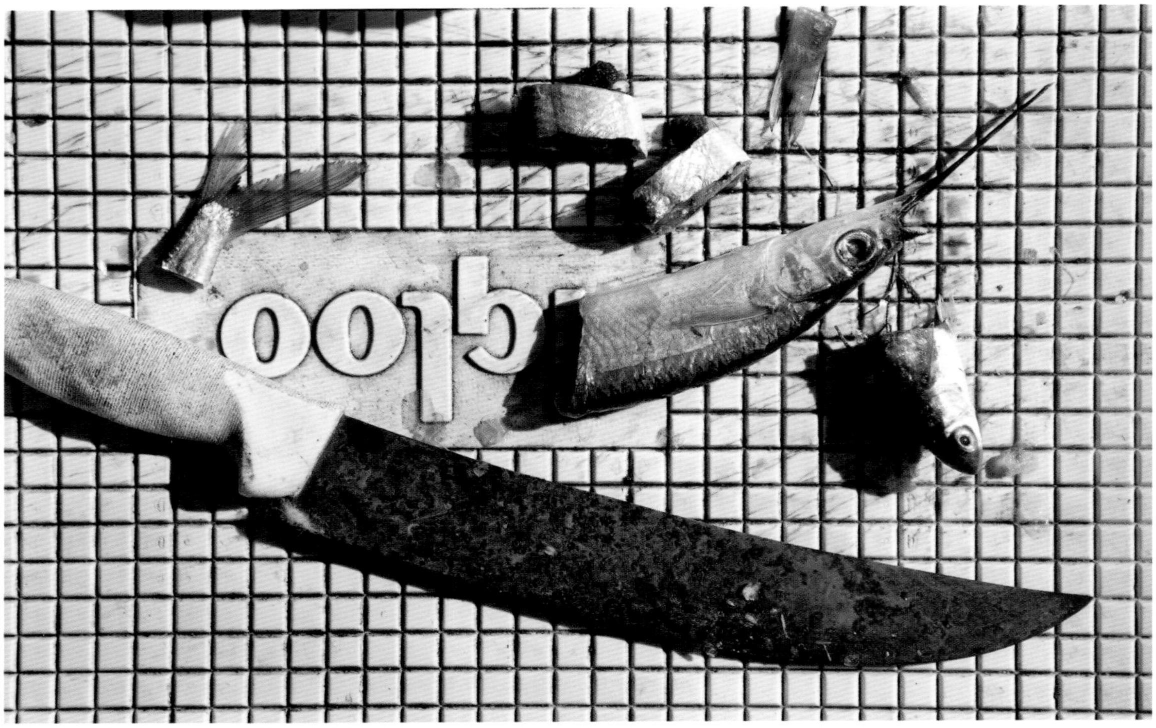

Hodgman

CAPT. ROY

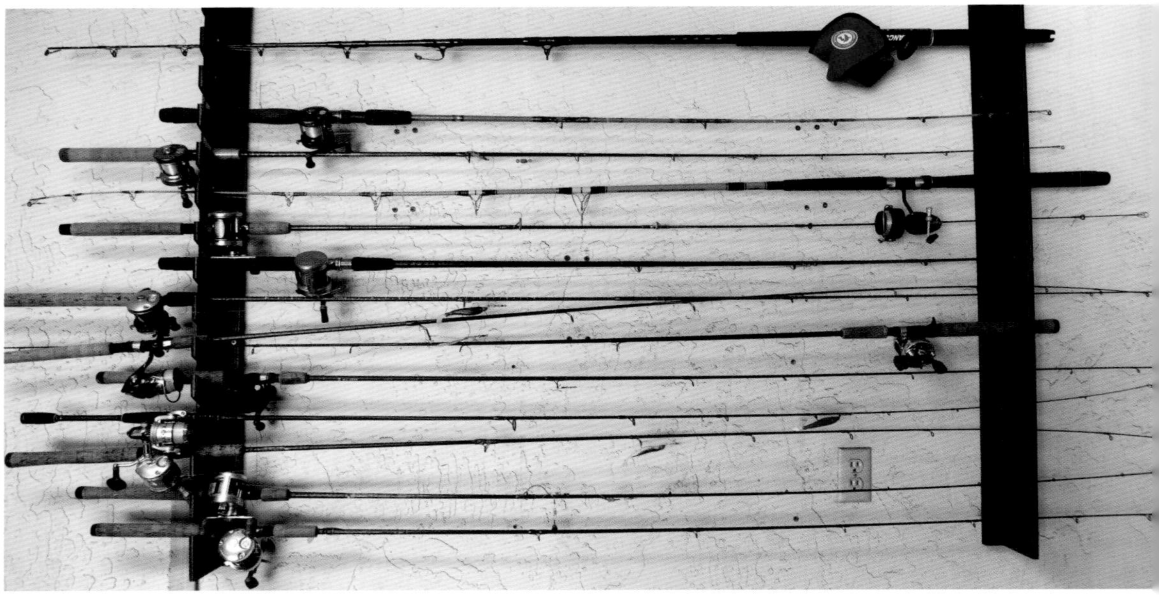

FISH AND
HOUSE GUESTS
STINK AFTER
THREE DAYS!
FISH ON!

FiSH

Redfish with Green Garlic Citrus Mojo

This is a dish that I love to make on the grill. What you want to do with fish is keep it simple. The days of overdoing it with butter sauces and stuff like that are over. We like fresh grilled fish with a good acid like lime and other citrus, and we try to take advantage of what's in season. We'll put redfish on the grill skin-side down, season it, and cover it, so it steams a little bit and gets smoky as well.

INGREDIENTS	MEASURE	CUT	PREPARATION
Grapefruit	1	Seeded and segmented	**For Green Garlic Citrus Mojo:** (1) In bowl combine first 3 ingredients, and set aside.
Orange	1	Seeded and segmented	
Mango Citrus Dressing *(see page 282)*	½ cup		
Green Garlic Ash *(see page 273)*	¼ cup	Chopped	(2) In saucepan on medium heat, slightly brown garlic in oil. (3) Stir in citrus mixture, and cook for approximately 1 minute.
Olive oil	¼ cup		
Redfish, skin on	2 sides		**For fish:** (4) Rub both sides with butter, salt, and pepper. (5) Grill fish skin-side down with lid closed 8 to 10 minutes. Do not flip. (6) Remove, place on platter, and immediately top with Mojo. Skin will come off easily for serving.
Butter	¼ cup, pads		
Salt and pepper	To taste

CHOICE
Big "C"
ORANGES
Houston, TX. 77007

RIO GRANDE VALLEY CITRUS

In the winter, when much of the beautiful Texas fruit is a distant seasonal memory, citrus is king. And not just the Ruby Red grapefruit so many people associate with Texas citrus production but a variety of oranges, lemons, and limes too. The rich sweetness they develop from sun-kissed groves in South Texas is balanced with a vibrant acidity that brightens any dessert, salad, or sauce.

I grew up in the Rio Grande Valley, which, in my opinion, grows some of the best citrus fruit in the world. Almost everybody had an orange tree or a grapefruit tree or a lime tree or a lemon tree in the yard. Being typical little kids, my friends and I had "citrus wars," where we pillaged fruit from neighborhood yards and met up before dark to throw them at each other.

Looking back, I see we were completely degrading what people were growing, and I know I'd be pretty ticked off if someone did that to my yard. But it was so plentiful that didn't even occur to us. It was always chilly when we were out picking the fruit off trees, which means it was late fall or winter when we were out messing around.

I don't think I knew anybody who harvested citrus, but you couldn't walk a corner in Brownsville without seeing bags of oranges or grapefruit for three dollars. I knew where it came from. The fruit was all around us. It wasn't uncommon for my mom to pick up a couple of bags on a regular basis. I loved to just peel and eat them. When I was lazy, I would cut 'em in half and suck out the juice.

Any time we ate tacos back home, which was pretty often, we had limes on hand. The limes down there were just a little bit smaller, like Mexican limes, and full of juice. We always had a big stash of them at home.

When I head down to South Texas toward the coast for some winter fishing, I make a stop at whatever roadside citrus stand is bursting with fresh picks. Save for picking something straight off the tree, those are the best spots for the freshest citrus. You'll often find a bit at farmers markets in Central Texas and you'll see bags of oranges and grapefruit lining grocery store shelves, but going straight to the Rio Grande Valley is how you guarantee you're getting the freshest fruit.

The South Texas subtropical climate, fertile soil, and sunny weather all provide excellent growing conditions. Texas citrus growers carefully maintain crop quality through successful irrigation techniques, growing conditions, and research.

The longer citrus hangs on the tree, the sweeter it gets, so early-season fruit is rarely the best. When you are looking for good citrus, choose the heaviest fruit for its size. That will carry the most juice. Once you get your citrus home, remove it from plastic, which encourages rotting, and store it in a cool place or in the refrigerator so it will last longest.

Eggnog Ice Cream

Gingerbread Cookies

Gingerbread Cookies

MAKES 20-30 COOKIES

Our pastry chef, Dee-Dee Sanchez, loves making cookies, and I'm a personal fan of the way she makes them because she likes them crispy like I do. There's nothing better than gingerbread cookies around the holidays. They have a great spiciness to them from the ginger, and they're fun to dip in frostings and chocolates for serving. If you have children, let them help you cut out different shapes and decorate them. Serve a couple cookies with a scoop or two of homemade Eggnog Ice Cream *(opposite)*. But be sure to leave a few just plain, because they are perfect for breakfast the next morning with a cup of coffee.

INGREDIENTS	MEASURE	CUT	PREPARATION
Brown sugar Butter	4 1/2 ounces 7 ounces		(1) In stand mixer with paddle attachment, cream together sugar and butter until light and fluffy.
Salt Ginger Cloves Allspice Cinnamon	Pinch 1 1/2 teaspoons 1 1/2 teaspoons 1 1/2 teaspoons 1 1/2 teaspoons		(2) In bowl, combine salt and 4 spices.
Molasses Honey, Texas Egg, Texas farm	3 ounces 2 ounces 1		(3) To butter mixture, add molasses, honey, and egg, blending thoroughly, scraping sides of bowl with spatula.
Flour, all-purpose Baking soda Water	1 1/2 pounds 1 teaspoon 3 tablespoons		(4) Add spice mixture and remaining ingredients, and mix until fully incorporated. (5) Wrap dough and refrigerate for at least 30 minutes. (6) Preheat oven to 350 degrees, then roll out dough to 1/4-inch thickness and use cookie cutters of your choice. (7) Bake on parchment-lined sheets, for approximately 7 minutes, then turn sheet and bake for 7 more minutes. For softer cookies, cook shorter; for crispier cookies, cook longer. (8) Decorate when cool.

Eggnog Ice Cream

SERVES 6-8

Eggnog is a staple at most holiday occasions. But sometimes it's hard to get people to pour a glass for themselves if it's just sitting at the bar. Somehow that's not a problem when you serve it for dessert in the form of ice cream. You don't have to spike it with bourbon, but it's a lot better if you do. Serve it with a couple of Gingerbread Cookies *(opposite)* to add a little spiciness.

INGREDIENTS	MEASURE	CUT		PREPARATION
Milk, whole	¾ cup			(1) In double boiler on stovetop, heat milk.
Sugar Cream cheese Mexican vanilla extract Eggs	¾ cup 4 ounces 1 teaspoon 2		**Add 2 tablespoons bourbon, if you like.*	(2) In stand mixer using paddle attachment, combine sugar with next 3 ingredients until smooth. (3) Temper in ¼ cup of heated milk, mixing until smooth, then transfer mixture into double boiler with milk. (4)Cook 5 to 10 minutes, stirring frequently with rubber spatula, until temperature reaches 165 degrees. (5) Cool to room temperature in ice bath.
Heavy cream Cinnamon Nutmeg	¾ cup ½ teaspoon 1 teaspoon	 Freshly grated		(6) Add cream, cinnamon, and nutmeg to mixture. (7) Process in ice-cream maker for 25 minutes, and freeze in airtight container 2 to 4 hours to harden.

Black-Bottom Pecan Sweet Potato Pie

Flourless Chocolate Torte

Black-Bottom Pecan Sweet Potato Pie

MAKES 2 PIES

If it sounds like this pie includes everything but the kitchen sink, that's because it does. You have people who love chocolate pie, pecan pie, and sweet potato pie (or pumpkin, if you would rather use that.) This is our way of pleasing everyone. Serve it warm or at room temperature, but I honestly like it chilled because the chocolate has a thicker texture, which layers with the creamy sweet-potato filling and the crunchy pecans—the best in layered texture and flavors.

INGREDIENTS	MEASURE	CUT	PREPARATION
Eggs	6		(1) With mixer in mixing bowl, combine first 4 ingredients until smooth.
Dark corn syrup	1½ cups		
Brown sugar	1½ cups		
Salt	½ teaspoon		
Dark rum	2 tablespoons		(2) Mix in rum, sweet potato, and vanilla.
Sweet potato, canned	1½ cups		
Vanilla	1 tablespoon		
Butter, melted	½ cups		(3) Preheat oven to 335 degrees. (4) Slowly add melted butter to mixture, and blend until smooth. (5) Lay chocolate chips and pecans onto piecrust bottoms, and divide filling between pies. (6) Place on sheet pan in oven, and bake for 35 to 45 minutes, until solid and golden brown.
Chocolate chips	1½ cups		
Pecan halves	3 cups		
Piecrusts	2		
Whipped cream	Dollop per serving		(7) Serve at room temperature with dollop of whipped cream.

Flourless Chocolate Torte

SERVES 6-8

If you love chocolate, skip plain old chocolate cake and go for a torte. It's richer and denser, almost like a fudge or a nice creamy chocolate bar, because it doesn't have any flour. It's also a great option if you serve people who are gluten intolerant. The key is to use a really nice semisweet chocolate for the glaze.

INGREDIENTS	MEASURE	CUT	PREPARATION
Dark chocolate Butter Sugar Brewed coffee, hot	1 pound 12 ounces 2/3 cup 3/4 cup	Chopped into bite-size pieces Chopped in chunks	(1) Spray 9-inch-round cake pan with cooking spray and line bottom with parchment paper. (2) In double boiler on stovetop, stir together chocolate and next 3 ingredients with rubber spatula until melted. Do not allow to boil or torte will be grainy. (3) Remove from heat and stir until slightly cooled.
Eggs, Texas farm	3	Slightly beaten	(4) Preheat oven to 350 degrees. (5) When spatula leaves tracks in mixture, it is sufficiently cooled; stir in eggs until incorporated and pour into pan. (6) Place in water bath in oven, and bake for approximately 45 minutes, until center is set and springs back when lightly touched. (7) Cool completely in pan in refrigerator for at least 4 hours. (8) To unmold, heat pan bottom briefly over flame or electric burner, run knife around perimeter, and turn onto cardboard circle.
Heavy cream Texas honey	1 cup 3 ounces		**For ganache glaze:** (9) In heavy saucepan whisk cream and honey to boil.
Semisweet chocolate chunks	1 pound		(10) Place chocolate in bowl, and pour in hot cream mixture, stirring briskly until ganache is uniform rich dark color. (11) Allow to sit approximately 30 minutes, stirring occasionally, before glazing torte. (12) To glaze, pour around sides first, then center; tilt tort to side to pour off excess ganache, and refrigerate 30 minutes to set before placing on serving dish.

Syrups

Syrups are components of a lot of our seasonal dishes. You can keep the syrups in the fridge for a while and use for all sorts of purposes. *Fennel:* we make syrup and use the leftover to dehydrate for a crisp or a candy. *Habanero-mango:* the syrup adds mystery to a cocktail and an unexpected finish to grilled fish or salad. *Citrus:* this syrup stars in cocktails and is the mojo in the Green Garlic–Citrus Mojo. *Red wine:* we cook down red wine with sugar and orange juice, and it works really well with steak, pork chops, and venison.

Fennel Syrup

MAKES 1 JAR PLUS CANDY

INGREDIENTS	MEASURE	CUT		PREPARATION
Sugar Water	1 cup 1 cup		**Syrup can be refrigerated and used for up to 4 weeks.*	(1) In small saucepan, cook sugar in water on medium-high heat until dissolved, approximately 5 minutes.
Fennel stalks	1 ½ cup	Thinly sliced		(2) Add fennel, reduce heat to medium, and cook approximately 5 minutes, stirring gently until slightly crisp and tender. (3) Remove and strain, reserving liquid. (4) Preheat oven to 250 degrees, and line baking sheet with parchment paper or use silicon liner. (5) Bonus: For candy, bake fennel, evenly separated, for 35 to 40 minutes, until dry and slightly sticky. (6) For syrup, simmer reserved liquid until thickened and approximately 1 cup remains; allow to cool.

Habanero-Mango Syrup

MAKES 2 JARS

INGREDIENTS	MEASURE	CUT		PREPARATION
Habanero	1 tablespoon	Seeded and diced	**Syrup can be refrigerated and used for up to 4 weeks.*	(1) In stainless-steel saucepan, bring all ingredients to a boil, then lower heat to low and reduce until thickened and approximately 2 cups remain. (2) Allow to cool approximately 2 hours, and using immersion blender, mix until smooth.
Mango	1 cup	Peeled, seeded and diced		
Sugar	1 ½ cups			
Orange juice	1 cup			
Lemon juice	1 cup			

Citrus Syrup

MAKES 2 JARS

INGREDIENTS	MEASURE	CUT		PREPARATION
Sugar	1 ½ cup		**Syrup can be refrigerated and used for up to 4 weeks.*	(1) In stainless-steel saucepan, bring all ingredients to a boil, then lower heat to low and reduce until thickened and approximately 1 ¾ cups remain; allow to cool.
Orange juice	1 cup			
Lemon juice	1 cup			

Balsamic Syrup

MAKES 2 JARS

INGREDIENTS	MEASURE	CUT		PREPARATION
Red wine (your favorite leftover wine)	1 cup		**Syrup can be refrigerated and used for up to 4 weeks.*	(1) In stainless-steel saucepan, bring all ingredients to a boil, then lower heat to low and reduce until thickened and approximately 1 ¾ cups remain; allow to cool.
Red wine vinegar	1 cup			
Orange juice	1 cup			
Sugar	1 cup			

Balsamic Syrup

Habanero-Mango Syrup

Citrus Syrup

Fennel Syrup

Citrus Jelly

MAKES 6-8 JARS

In winter you have access to many types of citrus, from grapefruit and oranges to tangerines and lemons. And a lot of times it's hard to find a way to use all of it. Here is a way to preserve them. Just mix them all together for this jelly, and use it on breakfast toast or as a glaze for something like grilled chicken.

INGREDIENTS	MEASURE	CUT	PREPARATION
Oranges Grapefruit Lemons Limes	1 pound 1 pound ½ pound ½ pound		(1) Zest one of each fruit and reserve. (2) Cut fruit in half and each half into quarters. (3) Squeeze pieces over strainer into bowl; discard seeds. (4) Using knife, scrape out pulp, and add to bowl; do not include membranes.
Water Sugar Kosher salt	6 cups 6 cups 1 teaspoon		(5) In stainless-steel saucepan, simmer juice and pulp with remaining ingredients until thickened, approximately 1 hour. (6) Place in jars uncovered to cool, then add lid, and refrigerate up to 4 weeks.

Onion–Wild Mushroom Jelly

MAKES 3 JARS

This is a savory jelly and one that's really good for a crostini or bruschetta appetizer. Toast small slices of good bread, and slather it on there. Then top it with blue cheese and a thinly sliced chilled roast beef or steak. Or serve it alongside a nice grilled steak. It just adds a little elegance to the dish.

INGREDIENTS	MEASURE	CUT		PREPARATION
Vegetable oil Onion	3 tablespoons 4 cups	 Thin julienned		(1) In heavy-duty braising skillet, cook onions in oil on low heat for approximately 2 hours, stirring every 5 minutes, to caramelize onions. Do not burn.
Mushrooms, your favorite Garlic	4 cups 1 tablespoon	Diced Chopped		(2) Add mushrooms and garlic, and simmer for approximately 30 minutes.
Honey Sherry vinegar Red wine (your favorite leftover wine)	2 tablespoons ¼ cup ¾ cup			(3) Add honey, vinegar, and wine, and cook until dissolved.
Butter	3 tablespoons			(4) Remove from heat, and stir in butter until melted.
Salt and pepper	To taste		**Jelly can be refrigerated and used for up to 2 weeks.*	(5) Season, allow to cool, and refrigerate.

BROKEN ARROW RANCH AND DIAMOND H RANCH

AS TOLD BY CHRIS HUGHES

BROKEN ARROW is a 30-year-old company started by my father, Mike Hughes, a former commercial diver who had spent much of his career traveling the world. He founded, and is still a director, of the world's largest underwater service company, Oceaneering International, Inc. By the early 80s, he began looking for a different career path, something he could do in the Texas Hill Country, and he saw a market opportunity. He noticed venison and game meat was popular in his travels but virtually nonexistent in the U.S.—except on the tables of hunting families in Texas—and he knew of no domestic source of venison. At the same time, Texas ranchers needed to better manage their exotic populations because wildlife biologists feared that non-native deer and antelope would compete with native whitetail and mule deer for food.

My father realized he could perform a service for those ranchers by harvesting game animals and then selling the meat. It was a new frontier. Others across the country were starting to farm deer for meat, but Dad didn't want to do that. He believed it would negatively affect the quality of the meat.

Meanwhile, no regulations or laws in Texas stated a person couldn't harvest venison on ranches as a service. That also meant my father had to protect his ability to do it. So he did the legislative legwork to get laws passed that would create a framework for allowing Broken Arrow to exist. He worked with Rick Perry, then a congressman, for new classifications on non-native deer and antelope. As a general law, you are not able to harvest native deer, such as whitetail, to sell. That goes back to protective federal measures put in place following a period in the 1800s when hunters, trappers, and fur traders wiped out entire populations of native wildlife across the country.

My dad, Mike Hughes, helped pass a law that classified non-native deer and animals as livestock. It allowed ranches and property owners the right to buy or sell those animals just like they would cattle, sheep, or goats. It also made it possible for Broken Arrow to begin building relationships with ranchers to allow us to harvest those animals for meat sale.

The relationship is pretty straightforward: We pay ranchers for the animals we harvest. Over the years we've had a lot of ranchers need help with their overpopulation problems, and they ask how much we charge. But that's not how we work. We believe the animals we harvest have value, and we believe in paying for that value. So it comes as a surprise to them when we say, "The good news is that we'll pay you to help with your overpopulation problem."

On the other side of our business is a growing demand from chefs and restaurants across the country for venison to add to their menus. Venison has transitioned from being just seasonal, for fall and winter dishes, common with continental cuisine, to being accepted by more progressive chefs as a lean and versatile protein for all seasons.

Venison, by definition, is any meat from a deer or an antelope, including moose, elk, caribou, axis, sika, and nilgai. The term derives from the Latin word "venor," which means to hunt or pursue, so venison refers to any meat that is hunted. In the culinary world, venison is used broadly when chefs present something versatile like chili, stew, or sausage, but we also work with chefs who specifically want a certain kind of meat, like elk tenderloin or antelope filet.

Our biggest competition is New Zealand red deer venison, which commands more than 80 percent of the U.S. market and supplies the majority of Europe and Asia. We have grown our business to supply approximately 10 percent of the market share across the country. More than 30 percent of our business is in major Texas cities, and we supply a number of restaurants in big cities throughout the U.S. It helps that we're able to offer a variety of venison.

BECAUSE WE DON'T farm the animals, one of our biggest challenges is supply. When we go to a ranch, a few of us drive around in a truck with the rancher. When we see an animal we can harvest, we shoot it and then use a mobile electro-stimulation device, which aids in accelerating the animal through the process of rigor mortis. It is commonly used in slaughterhouses and helps tenderize the meat.

Many people would consider what we do to be hunting, and in a lot of ways it is. Personally, I enjoy hunting for the sport, but shooting an animal from a vehicle with the intent to take as many as possible isn't sport for me. Stalking and waiting for the right animal fits my definition of hunting a bit better. What we do is considered "fair chase" because we're taking an animal in its natural wild habitat. Sometimes we have a good day and can take as many as 30 animals. Other times, we may get only five or even none. It's not the most efficient process from a business standpoint, but it is the most humane. We want the animal to experience as little stress as possible and for it to be in its natural environment. It's the right thing to do, and it gives us the best quality meat.

Meat quality was an aspect of business my dad had to address. Typically, in a slaughterhouse a state inspector is on site to inspect the meat when it's being processed. You have to build your facility and have it inspected according to state and federal standards. But with wild animals, we knew trapping would induce stress and affect meat quality, so instead of bringing the animals to the plant to slaughter, we had to bring the plant to the animals. There was no precedent for field harvesting with a mobile processing unit. But we built one on a trailer according to specifications, brought it up for inspection, and received the first government approval for a mobile processing plant. We have a state inspector with us at the time of processing.

When I was growing up, I worked with the family company a little. There was a time when we'd even take chefs out for hunts. I was about 13 years old, and I drove them out to their deer blinds, took them food, and picked them up at the end of the hunt. But when I was 18, like many kids graduating high school—especially in a small town like Ingram—I didn't really have a vision of being part of the family business. Instead, I went to Tennessee to get an engineering degree. Later I worked in advertising and engineering firms that allowed my wife and me to live overseas in the Balkans. But ultimately we came home, because we both felt that raising a family in the Texas Hill Country was pretty hard to beat.

My dad loved the idea. He was already pushing back from daily operations in anticipation of retiring. So in 2005, I took over.

One of the things we've tried to concentrate on as a business is not becoming a novelty purveyor. We get asked to work with specific types of meat and expand our portfolio, but oftentimes you end up losing focus on what you're good at. It becomes about novelty, not quality. At the same time, though, we are a supply-constrained business. The methods we use for harvesting are self-limiting: We work with only so many places, and harvests vary.

So we experimented over the years with options such as wild boar. But in 2010 we stumbled on something that became a really good fit. A gentleman who owned a ranch in Bandera, Diamond H Ranch, a quail-farming business, wanted to retire. So we did our due diligence and bought it. It's a pretty unique business in that we work with two species for two markets. We raise coturnix quail to harvest and sell to restaurants for meat, and we raise bobwhite quail to sell to ranches for hunting and to repopulate their land. Our facility has a hatchery in which we produce and incubate the eggs, and we grow all the quail on site. We process the coturnix quail there too, which is unusual—but again, we do that to reduce stress on the bird. We also sell quail eggs to restaurants.

When Dad started all this, he had no notion it would still be going 30 years later. We try to do things as sustainably as possible, which benefits our overall quality. Our philosophy is that happy birds make tasty birds. At Diamond H, we use a local mill for feed, compost all of our litter and manure, which we sell to local landscaping companies, and use no antibiotics or medications on the birds. We're shooting for another 30 years.

We want the animal to experience as little stress as possible and for it to be in its natural environment.

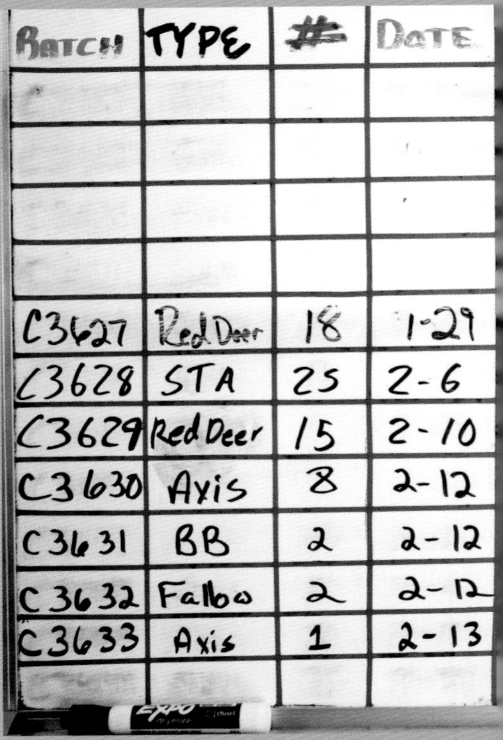
BATCH TYPE # DATE
C3627 Red Deer 18 1-29
C3628 STA 25 2-6
C3629 Red Deer 15 2-10
C3630 Axis 8 2-12
C3631 BB 2 2-12
C3632 Fallow 2 2-12
C3633 Axis 1 2-13

BROKEN ARROW RANCH

CHRIS TENEYCK

Working in restaurants is something I just stumbled into. I started picking up shifts at places in North Austin when I was about 17 and got my foot in the door just to understand how a kitchen works. What kept me there was a passion for food. As it turns out, I needed the kitchen to balance me out. I was a very active and hyper teenager, and I thrived on the type of hard work the kitchen afforded me.

I eventually found my way into the kitchen at Z Tejas at the Arboretum when I was about 19, and Jack really brought me under his wing. It was a gift, like going to culinary school right on the job. Since then, he's been a father figure to me. Not only is he an extremely talented chef and a great businessman, but he has taught me values and life lessons outside of the kitchen.

By the time I had grown through the ranks, Jack promoted me to open the location at Avery Ranch, north of Austin. Soon after that I heard rumors of his leaving to start something on his own. I figured he would have chefs from all over the place in line to come work for him. So I waited a while to see how things would play out. Finally I got the nerve to sit him down and talk to him.

I told him about the rumors and said if there was any way I could be a part of it—whether it was as a grill cook or whatever— I was interested. He looked me in the eye and said, "Are you kidding? I want you to be my number-one guy."

I was floored. Opening the first Jack Allen's Kitchen was an amazing experience. Coming into it, I didn't know what to expect. We had a vision for what we wanted to do. But it was the first time I had been challenged to bring local farmers into the fold and grow my culinary skills to be creative with seasonal ingredients on a regular basis. Jack really let me lead the way, and it changed my whole view on cooking.

The experience has also taught me a lot about crediting the farmers for what they do. They work hard and oftentimes just the chefs get in the limelight. My job is to elevate what they have done in the field so that it's delicious and approachable for our guests.

It's been a cool journey for me over the past decade. People ask me if I ever want to have my own place, but that's on the way back burner. Jack and his team are really important to me. They're my family, and that's not just something you walk away from.

ANTONIO "ROJO" LUJANO

If you had told me 15 years ago that one day I would be running the kitchen of a 340-seat restaurant in Austin, I wouldn't have believed you. At that time, I was elbow-deep in soapy water, working as a dishwasher at Z Tejas in the Arboretum. Dishwasher was the first job I could get at 16, but since day one, I knew I wanted to cook. I used to look at the sous chefs and head chefs and think, "Someday, I'll be one of them."

It took me a few years, but I eventually became a sous chef. I had a chance to learn a lot about cooking from Jack and the other chefs. I spent three years in that spot and was able to really grow my skills and understand how to be creative with cooking.

Around that same time, I was offered the head chef position at a new location in San Antonio. It was an offer I couldn't pass up, even though I hated to leave my family and friends. I worked hard during that first year, and one day Jack came in to see me. By then, Jack Allen's Kitchen had been open for a couple of years, and he asked me to come work for him. It wasn't an easy decision. I loved working with him, but I had such a great job in San Antonio. I told him I needed to think about it.

I'm lucky he's a persistent man, because he had to bug me for a few months before I finally agreed.

In October 2011, I joined the Jack Allen's team. I learned my way around the kitchen pretty quickly, but I'd never been to farmers markets. Jack had me going every weekend to stock up on what I needed for a few days. It was a new way of doing things for me, and I loved it.

I've had a chance to become friends with the farmers and purveyors and even get out to their farms on my days off. The best part is I'm working with what I consider my family. If I have a problem, I go to Jack or Tom. If my cooks need something, they come to me.

I love what I do. People ask me if I take some sort of happy drug because I'm always smiling when I get to work. I wouldn't want to be anywhere else. There are a lot of restaurants I could work for—big or small—but the concept we have here and our method is different from anywhere else.

I have dreams like everybody. Maybe one day, years from now, I'll have a restaurant of my own, but it won't be without Jack Gilmore's blessing and support.

DEE-DEE SANCHEZ

I've been baking ever since I was a young girl. My mom was a teacher, and baking was one of those interactive things we could do together. We made cakes and cookies that I'd sell in bake sales. I grew up in Lansing, Michigan, but my parents were from the Rio Grande Valley of Texas and eventually moved back there when they retired to get away from the cold. I spent 11 years in Denver, where I got a degree in culinary management at the Art Institute of Colorado. I learned both the savory and sweet sides of cooking, but my heart has always been in pastry cooking. It's always just come more naturally to me.

When I'd leave the mountains to visit my parents in Texas for holidays and vacations, I finally realized I wanted to live closer to family. My sister and cousin both lived in Austin, and I figured out pretty quickly that's where I wanted to be too. I moved down in November 2007 and got a job at a place called the Cake Plate, where I was the lead cake decorator for a couple of years. Then I heard about this new restaurant in Oak Hill that was about to open and needed a part-time pastry chef.

I managed to get an interview with Jack Gilmore, and he described the type of food he was doing for Jack Allen's and the sort of desserts he wanted to serve. Then he asked me to bring desserts to a tasting the following week. He told me a few things to steer clear of and that he really didn't like banana desserts or anything with bananas involved.

So I brought him a large dark chocolate truffle called the Chocolate Bomb and a Banana Toffee Pie. He ate the whole thing. Then he looked at me and said, "Girl, you've got balls. You're hired!"

I started out working part-time, but we eventually realized I was going to need to be around a lot more. I usually have about five desserts on the menu at a time. A few of them are permanent, like the Chocolate Bomb and the Blondie Brownie Pie, which is a variation of a recipe I learned when I lived up north. But I also try to keep a few seasonal items on deck, just like Jack does with the main menu. The summers give us stone fruit and berries, and in the fall, we transition to apples, pears, and figs. The winter is great for citrus, and in the spring, I most look forward to strawberries.

Personally, I love making cakes. Big layer cakes. But my favorite thing is cookies. I'll make just about any kind of cookie. Since we've grown to another location, I've been able to hire a couple of assistants, which has allowed me time to be creative with new ideas and stay organized about what we're rotating on the menu. Of course, I manage to weave in that famous Banana Toffee Pie a few times a year—and it sells out every time.

DAVID TOBY

I started tending bar when I was 19. It was at a microbrewery in downtown Austin called the Copper Tank, which held a sort of iconic status back in its heyday. That was when I was in college at the University of Texas. I grew up in Dallas, but once I got to Austin for college, I knew it was a place I wanted to call home. I finished school at Texas Tech University in Lubbock and had a chance to work in Minnesota for a few years as a general manager for a chain of sports bars. It was a great experience, but I really wanted to get back to Austin. More than that, I wanted to work in an environment that required less of the late-night lifestyle, something more suited for a long-term career.

So I made the move back to Austin. I was solidifying a commitment to manage a well-known seafood and steak restaurant when a friend I worked with at the Copper Tank suggested I talk to his friends who were opening a restaurant in Oak Hill.

When you sit down with Tom and Jack and get them talking about their vision and goals, you can't help but want a piece of it. They just have this infectious energy that is hard to escape. Thirty minutes into the conversation with them, I excused myself and called the other restaurant to let them know I'd decided to take another path. There was just something about the idea of starting with a couple of guys who were locally focused and wanted to do a new concept of their own.

Tom made the decision for me pretty clear when he said, "Do you want to work at a place where you can have fun, manage things your way, and have your ideas heard, or do you want to work in a more corporate environment where the regimen is set in stone and you have to wear a suit every day?"

I signed on to be the beverage manager for the company and bar manager for the Oak Hill location. My primary job is to run the bar program as far as what beer, wine, and spirits we carry, and also make sure all of our locations stay consistent. I work with Tom to get his input on things, because he has his eye on the overall operations of the business, but I take responsibility for the beverage side of things.

I love getting to work with a global selection of beer, wine, and spirits, but it's been even more exciting to work with the producers in Texas, who are making some amazing products that we can all be really proud of and enjoy.

INDEX

Italic page numbers refer to photographs.

D

E

PHOTO CREDITS

ALL PHOTOGRAPHY BY KENNY BRAUN

With the exception of:
LuAnn Gilmore: page 7, page 8 (#1 and #6); Shannon Coletti: page 8 (#4); Mike Curran: page 8 (#2); Jessica Dupuy: pages 28, 260 (middle right); Sarah Teveldal: page 140; Holly Jackson *Austin American-Statesman*: page 105; Laura Merians: page 184 (bottom right image); Unknown: page 151; Bob Stickney: page 184 (top left); Laura Merians: page 184 (bottom right).

Food Styling by Meghan Erwin
Copyediting by Dana Frank

OAK HILL, GKSD RESTAURANT ENTERPRISES, LLC
7720 Highway 71 W.
Austin, Texas 78735
jackallenskitchen.com

Library of Congress Control Number: 2014907349

Printed in China through Asia Pacific Offset
First Edition, 2014

Text set in Chronicle Text and Wilma

Book and cover design by
Julie Savasky and DJ Stout
Pentagram Design, Austin, Texas

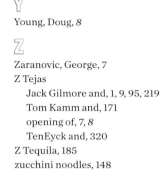

FRIENDS OF JAK

FARMERS AND PURVEYORS

Amador Farms
Animal Farm
B5 Farm
Bat Creek Farm
Bee Creek Farms
Bella Verdi
Boggy Creek Farms
Brazos Valley Cheese
Broken Arrow Ranch
Buena Tierra
Caeda Farm
Celtic Seafare
Cocoa Puro Chocolates
Dewberry Hills Farm
Diamond H Ranch
Dos Lunas Artisan Cheeses
Eagle Mountain Cheese
Eden's Cove Farm
Engel Farm
Farm to Table
Fiesta Tortillas
Fikes Family Farms
Flintrock Farm
Fruitful Hill Farm
Full Quiver Farms
G & S Orchards
Garza Gardens Herbs
Hairston Creek Farm
Harvest Time Farm Stand
Hat Creek Pickle Company
Hillside Farm
I O Ranch Lamb
Indian Hills Farm
J & B Farms
Johnson's Backyard
Katz Coffee Roasters
Lightsey Farms
Milagro Farms
Mill King Market & Creamery
Mozzarella Company
Naegelin Farms
Oak Hill Farms
Oma & Opa Farms
Ottmers Family Farm
Our Fathers Farm
Pasta and Company
Peach Creek Farm
Pedernales Valley Farms
Pure Luck Farm
Quality Seafood
Richardson Farms
Rinnger Farms
Rockin' B Ranch
Round Rock Honey
San Saba Pecans
Simmons Family Farms
Swede Farm
Tecolote Organic Farm
Texas Hill Country Olive Company
Texas Olive Ranch
Thunderheart Bison
Twin County Dorpers
Two Happy Children Farm
Urban Roots
Winters Family Farm
Wood Duck Farm

WINERIES

Brennan Vineyards
Becker Vineyards
Driftwood Estate Vineyards
Duchman Family Winery
Fall Creek Vineyards
Flat Creek Estate
Messina Hoff Winery
McPherson Cellars
Pedernales Cellars
William Chris Vineyards

SPIRITS

512 Tequila
Balcones Distilling
Cinco Vodka
Cypress Creek Rum
Deep Eddy Vodka
Dripping Springs Vodka
Dulce Vida Organic Tequila
Enchanted Rock Vodka
Firestone and Robertson Distilling
Garrison Brothers Texas Straight Bourbon Whiskey
Genius Gin
Paula's Texas Spirits
Rebecca Creek Whiskey
Republic Tequila
Savvy Vodka
Tito's Handmade Vodka
Treaty Oak Distilling
White Hat Rum
Z Tequila

BREWERIES

(512) Brewing Company
Austin Beerworks
Circle Brewing
Hops and Grain
Independence Brewing Company
Live Oak Brewing Company
Rahr & Sons
Real Ale Brewing Company
Rogness Brewing Company
Spoetzl Brewery
Thirsty Planet Brewing Company

The hard part about trying to create a complete list of the farmers and purveyors we work with is that I know there will be someone missing. We're always welcoming new friends into our family and hope to continue to do so. Without all of the hard work that all of you do, Jack Allen's Kitchen wouldn't be what it is today. And for that, we thank you.

Jack Allen's Kitchen